Plymouth

Vision of a modern city

Plymouth

Vision of a modern city

Jeremy Gould

Published by English Heritage, Kemble Drive, Swindon SN2 2GZ
www.english-heritage.org.uk
English Heritage is the Government's statutory adviser on all aspects of the historic environment.

First published 2010

ISBN 978 1 84802 050 4
Product code 51531

British Library Cataloguing in Publication Data
A CIP catalogue record for this book is available from the British Library.

Typeset in ITC Charter 9.25pt on 13pt

Photographs by Peter Williams and Jeremy Gould
Aerial photographs by Damian Grady
Graphics by Philip Sinton
Brought to publication by Jess Ward, Publishing, English Heritage
Edited by Susan Kelleher
Page layout by George Hammond
Printed in Belgium by DeckersSnoeck

Contents

Acknowledgements

Jeremy Gould is an architect and architectural historian and Emeritus Professor of Architecture at the University of Plymouth. This book is based on research initially commissioned by Plymouth City Council from Jeremy & Caroline Gould Architects in 1999 and presented to the city in 2000 as *Plymouth Planned: The Architecture of the Plan for Plymouth 1943–1962*. This focussed on the city centre but more recent research commissioned by English Heritage has expanded to include the Plymouth suburbs and the city centres of Exeter, Bristol and Coventry. The author would like to thank the following who have made valuable contributions to the research: Kenneth Bingham; Neil Emery; Dr Stephen Essex, University of Plymouth; Peter Ford, Plymouth City Council; Caroline Gould; Dr Elain Harwood, English Heritage; Gareth Hughes; Library of the Royal Institute of British Architects; Local Studies Library Plymouth City Council; David Mackay; Dr Daniel Maudlin, University of Plymouth; Hilary Phillips on Ernesettle; Plymouth and West Devon Record Office; Graham Thorne; University of Plymouth Library.

The author would also like to thank Colum Giles, Head of Urban Research at English Heritage, for his help and advice in editing the work and English Heritage staff for providing illustrations: Damian Grady took the aerial photographs, Peter Williams took most of the ground photographs and Philip Sinton provided the maps.

Foreword

Britain's recovery from the Second World War was long, slow and painful, but there were many outstanding achievements in the decades after 1945. The rebuilding of the cities damaged by bombing amounted to one of the most radical changes to the urban environment that the country had witnessed for many centuries: perhaps only the reconstruction of London after the Great Fire in 1666 bears comparison with what happened in Coventry, Exeter and other ravaged towns. Plymouth, however, is the most spectacular example of how the opportunities presented by wartime damage were grasped by a new breed of visionary town planners to produce an environment for the modern age, bright, clean, spacious and in tune with the optimism of the post-war years.

Not everyone liked the new Plymouth as it was being built. The city is now over half a century old and, inevitably, the years have taken their toll. Renewal is again needed to allow Plymouth to serve the needs of its people, and the part to be played by the legacy of the post-war years is the focus of debate. Decisions must be taken for the future, and they must be based upon a sound understanding of what is important in the existing landscape. This book sets out such an assessment. It may challenge many deeply held views, but it also allows us to see the city in a new light, informed by a better awareness of how Abercrombie's plan reflected the ideals of an extraordinary period in our history. English Heritage offers this assessment as part of its contribution to the discussion of what 21st-century Plymouth should be.

English Heritage is very grateful to the University of Plymouth, and in particular to Professor Jeremy Gould, for their help in producing this book. It is very important that we present the most authoritative view of the historic environment, and this collaboration has allowed us to do this in this case. English Heritage will continue to work closely with Plymouth City Council in developing and executing a new vision. Our role is to raise awareness of the importance of Plymouth's historic environment, help people to appreciate what it represents, and work with partners to give it new life in a city which meets modern needs.

Baroness Andrews, Chair, English Heritage

1

The plan for Plymouth

In the autumn of 1941, Plymouth City Council appointed Professor Patrick Abercrombie to prepare a plan for the new city of Plymouth. Abercrombie was the most distinguished town planner of his generation. He was trained as an architect but had become professor of civic design at Liverpool University in 1915 and professor of town planning at London University in 1935. He was founding editor of the influential *Town Planning Review* and in the 1920s and 1930s had prepared a series of regional planning studies through which he invented and perfected a system of planning consisting of analysis, synthesis and practical proposition which established his international reputation. He had just been commissioned by Lord Reith, Minister of Works and Buildings, to prepare the *County of London Plan*, the first of the national reconstruction plans.

The city that Abercrombie inherited lay in ruins. The Second World War had brought the front line to British cities as never before. The first bombs fell on Plymouth in July 1940 and the last in April 1944, just before D-Day, although the main damage to the city centre was inflicted in 1941 (Fig 1). More than 1,000 civilians were killed and a further 3,000 injured. The military casualties were never admitted. The damage to buildings was considerable – Plymouth was the most devastated city in England. Almost 4,000 houses were destroyed and a further 18,000 seriously damaged and 20,000 people were displaced. The greatest damage was to the area around the civic centre where the department stores, the municipal buildings and Guildhall Square were destroyed leaving St Andrew's Church and the Guildhall itself as roofless shells. The bomb maps and contemporary photographs reveal that the damage was uneven, leaving many structures intact or at least repairable, but, in an important garrison, a city in ruins was unacceptable and perceived to be bad for morale. The Royal Navy cleared the streets of rubble and James Paton Watson, the city engineer and surveyor, closed the city centre for one month while the Royal Engineers dynamited and removed the remaining buildings, which were considered unsafe. The population of the city centre fell to just over half its pre-war total and the city's rate income fell by one third. Around the old street pattern from Derry's Cross to St Andrew's Cross and south to Notte Street spread a vast triangular cleared space of 114 acres (46.13 ha), surrounded by damaged buildings. The Naval Memorial on the Hoe was visible for the first time across the derelict space of Princess Square.

Plymouth city centre bomb damage after clearance, 1947. The trees of Westwell Street gardens (centre), with the ruined Guildhall and St Andrew's Church (centre left). Slum housing remains (bottom right). [NMR/aflo03/aerofilms/a7572]

Figure 1
St Andrew's Church tower and nave seen
through the ruins of the Municipal Offices on
Bedford Street, with the Guildhall (right),
c 1941.
[Reproduced by permission of the Plymouth
and West Devon Record Office, Plymouth
Library Service and the Plymouth Herald,
P000073954]

Plymouth before the war – a Victorian city

A visitor to Plymouth in the late 1930s would have witnessed a city almost unchanged by the 20th century. It was a flourishing, commercial city based on shipping and fishing and on the Royal Naval dockyard at Devonport which employed some 12,000 of its 220,000 inhabitants, making it the largest city on the Channel coast. It had become a city officially in 1928, formed from the separate towns of Plymouth, Stonehouse and Devonport. The three towns saw themselves as rivals so that the amenities, institutions, shopping, entertainments and housing were spread more or less evenly across the city from the docks on the River Tamar at Devonport in the west to the fishing harbour of the Barbican and the estuary of the River Plym in the east. The three towns had grown organically, restrained only by the commercial uses along the waters' edge, the needs of the Navy and Army and the hilly topography. Most of the buildings were architecturally modest, a mixture of Regency and Victorian styles and the grand architectural gestures were reserved for the military – the Citadel, the Royal Naval Hospital, Stonehouse Barracks, the Royal William Yard and the other dockyard buildings up the edge of the Tamar.

There had been one significant attempt to give the three towns some civic grandeur. John Foulston, Plymouth's major Regency architect, had designed Union Street which connected Devonport to Plymouth in a single east–west axis in 1820. This terminated in the Town Hall and column at Devonport and set up a series of symmetrical spaces of which only the Octagon in Stonehouse was built in the consistent style intended. Foulston was responsible for two other set pieces in Plymouth – Princess Square and the Crescent – and for the grandest of the new institutions – the Theatre Royal, the Athenaeum and St Catherine's Church – all in the neo-Grecian manner. But architectural fashions changed and, later in the century, the new civic buildings adjacent to St Andrew's Church, the Guildhall and the civic offices around Guildhall Square, were in a flamboyant medieval Gothic style built in the local grey limestone, and Alfred Waterhouse designed the offices for Prudential Assurance – also Gothic but in red terracotta (Fig 2). Plymouth was a crowded city; there were few open

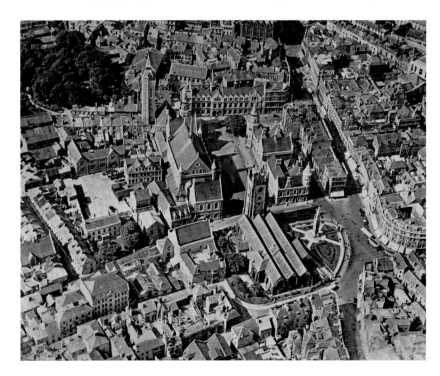

Figure 2
Aerial view of Plymouth centred on Guildhall
Square before 1939 from A Plan for Plymouth.
The Guildhall (centre left) and Municipal Buildings
(centre right) with St Andrew's Church and
St Andrew's Cross (lower right).
[Abercrombie and Paton Watson 1943, frontispiece.
Reproduced by permission of the Plymouth and
West Devon Record Office, Ref 1655]

spaces except for Central Park, north of the railway station, and the Hoe, overlooking Plymouth Sound. The Hoe was the city's pleasure ground and served the burgeoning tourist industry. The Naval Memorial designed by Sir Robert Lorimer had been built here in the 1920s and below it, on the foreshore adjacent to the Victorian pier, the art-deco Tinside Lido was added in 1929–35. Elsewhere, the demands of popular entertainment required the demolition of older buildings. The Theatre Royal was replaced by the Royal Cinema in 1937 and somehow the vast Regent and Gaumont cinemas were slotted into Frankfort Street and Union Street respectively.

The crowded city meant that it was very difficult for new development to keep pace with demands. The department stores were crammed into Bedford Street and Spooner's store had expanded into various buildings around St Andrew's Cross. Dingles, the city's largest department store, was wanting to redevelop but could not buy a site of sufficient area. Worst of all, the city streets were dangerously full of traffic – delivery vehicles, private cars and motorbuses, which had almost replaced the decrepit tramway and trolley buses, vied with pedestrians who overflowed the narrow pavements. Princess Square had been turned into the city's first car park; one-way traffic systems had been introduced and through traffic, heading for the Torpoint ferry and Cornwall, clogged the constricted streets and Union Street. The traffic at St Andrew's Cross was said to be the highest density in southern England outside London. Paton Watson, who had been appointed in 1936, had tried unsuccessfully to implement road-widening schemes for which the negotiations for compensation were both protracted and expensive. There was a crisis in housing too. Much of the housing of Devonport, Stonehouse and the Barbican was hardly better than slums. Although some new council flats had been built in the Barbican and model housing in the suburbs, for example by the Astor family at Mount Gould, the city faced a major programme of new housing for which it had neither the resources nor the land.

Through the Blitz Plymothians seemed indomitable. Morale was high – King George VI and Queen Elizabeth visited in March 1941 and Winston Churchill in May. Lord Reith followed in July at the invitation of the wartime mayor, Lord Astor, and his wife Nancy, the Member of Parliament for Plymouth Sutton. Reith urged the city council to prepare a plan for reconstruction and to plan 'boldly and comprehensively' in order to be ready for what government funds might be available after the war. Although this was a standard speech given to other cities and was mostly an encouragement to the war effort, there was a growing realisation that the Blitz may have given cities an opportunity to solve problems that had seemed insuperable. There was huge public interest in town planning – many popular books on the subject became best-sellers (including Abercrombie's *Town & Country Planning*, reprinted in 1943) and the Government sponsored a touring exhibition, *Living in Cities* in 1940–1, which promoted far-reaching solutions to city planning and promised a bright, new, clean future. The Astors were keenly interested in social reform and public health and were determined to influence their city. No doubt they and the council also realised that in appointing Abercrombie, they were buying both a radical new plan and valuable political connections. It was clear in 1941 that the old city was not going to be recreated.

Patrick Abercrombie and *A Plan for Plymouth*

Figure 3
Patrick Abercrombie and James Paton Watson presenting A Plan for Plymouth, c 1944 – *(left to right) James Paton Watson, Colin Campbell (town clerk), Patrick Abercrombie, Lord Astor (mayor) and Bill Modley (deputy mayor). [Reproduced by permission of the Plymouth and West Devon Record Office, 1418/02011]*

A Plan for Plymouth under the joint authorship of Abercrombie and Paton Watson was published in March 1944 (although dated 1943) (Fig 3). It did not disappoint. The handsome volume first analysed the history, topography, geography, demography and communications of the greater city area and then set out principles of new development for the countryside, suburbs and city centre. The principles for the countryside and suburbs fit comfortably within contemporary ideas expressed by the Council for the Preservation of Rural England (which Abercrombie had jointly founded) and others: the countryside was for both agriculture *and* for recreation, existing villages were admired and left alone and the limits of suburban growth were carefully fixed. The existing and new suburbs were split into 'neighbourhood units' of between 6,000 and 10,000 people, each with its own 'neighbourhood centre' containing 'community buildings' gathered together in a 'precinct'.

The idea of the 'precinct' was fundamental to the whole plan. It was borrowed from H Alker Tripp, the assistant commissioner of the Metropolitan police, who in his *Town Planning and Road Traffic* (1942) proposed a hierarchy of main traffic routes that kept high-speed through traffic away from shopping and residential areas or precincts. Thus the A38 trunk road from Exeter was

Figure 4
City centre plan from A Plan for Plymouth.
[Abercrombie and Paton Watson 1943, 66.
Reproduced by permission of the Plymouth
and West Devon Record Office, Ref 1655]

extended westwards like an American 'parkway', away from the neighbourhoods to a new road crossing over the River Tamar adjacent to Brunel's railway bridge. The city centre became a series of precincts, surrounded by a gyratory traffic system which connected the old A38, the roads to the northern suburbs and the route to the Torpoint ferry along Union Street, now a dual carriageway. This was no longer a shopping street because, according to Tripp, 'it is wrong to lead the heavy traffic-flows through places where shopping crowds congregate'.[1]

The proposal for the city centre within this gyratory system was truly radical. Abercrombie erased the whole of the old centre, its streets and most of its buildings and then drew a grand axis through them from the Naval Memorial on the Hoe to the railway station at North Hill. He declared the space a 'vista' for public enjoyment 'to be enriched by the landscape architect's and gardener's art' (Fig 4).[2] Across the axis he composed a series of streets running east–west and between them he allocated the functions of the precincts – government and offices in the north, the shopping precinct in the centre, the civic centre, and hotel and residential adjacent to the Hoe. To the east, the Barbican harbour precinct was labelled 'historic Plymouth'; to the west, between Union Street and Millbay docks, 'industry' with a stadium and 'marine pavilion' behind Millbay station; to the north, the main railway station and bus station with cultural centre to its east, reinforcing the existing museum and art gallery with BBC studios, health centre and public baths (Fig 5). The civic centre preserved only St Andrew's and the Prysten House, and part of Foulston's Crescent from the old city. Now he added new municipal offices, council chamber, law courts, Guildhall, banks and, on the western side, a theatre and cinema, rebuilt from the old Royal Cinema, and a market. The road intersections around the perimeter, the intersections of the main and cross axes and the road ends of the shopping precinct were expressed as clear geometrical shapes – ellipses, circles, semicircles and octagons and the whole composition was engineered to be almost symmetrical about the main axis. Of the old streets, only Union Street was integrated with the new layout. The scale of old Plymouth was swept away, to be replaced by something very much grander. The width of the main axis was 200ft (61m), the main cross axis 175ft (53.3m) with a garden between the carriageways of 75ft (22.9). The new city centre covered 193 acres (78.1ha) of which only 12 per cent was shopping

Figure 5
City centre zoning diagram from A Plan for Plymouth.
[Abercrombie and Paton Watson 1943, 71. Reproduced by permission of the Plymouth and West Devon Record Office, Ref 1655]

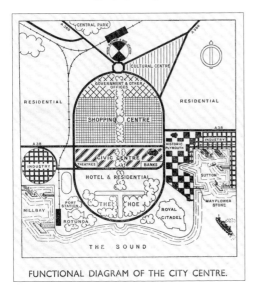

(an increase of 40 per cent from the old centre), 3.5 per cent civic centre,
14 per cent cultural precinct, 9 per cent offices and banks, 9 per cent residential
and hotels, 11.5 per cent open space and 31 per cent roads.[3]

Plymouth was Abercrombie's largest and most ambitious plan. He had
not attempted anything on this scale before and one must look elsewhere
for its precedents. Like many of his generation, his training had been in the
Beaux-Arts, the French system of architecture and planning which was taught
in the 19th century at the École des Beaux-Arts in Paris. It formed the basis
of most architectural education in Europe and America and at the Liverpool
School of Architecture where he taught, with its emphasis on classicism,
symmetry, pure geometrical shapes and linear axes as generators of plan
forms. He had a predilection for formal plans, Scamozzi's ideal town, L'Enfant's
Washington and Palma Nova (1593) in the state of Venice, for example, and
he had written that 'the grid iron road plan was that least elevated but most
honourably ancient form'.[4] There are allusions to the gridded Georgian plan
of Edinburgh New Town and its relationship to the older city. The main cross
street at Plymouth, Royal Parade, is similar in composition to Princes Street
in Edinburgh and it too terminates in significant buildings. The scale of the
gyratory road and its intersections have similarities to the great Beaux-Arts
plans of the early century – Edwin Lutyens's plan for New Delhi (1912) (Fig 6)
and Walter Burley Griffin's plan for Canberra (1912), both of which had been
discussed in the *Town Planning Review*. The main axis and the idea of creating
a park-like centre is very similar to Welwyn Garden City in Hertfordshire,
planned in 1920, and it is no coincidence that the great greensward, Parkway,
at Welwyn was also 200ft (61m) wide. The illustrations in the *Plan* by the
perspectivist J D M Harvey imply a city *en fête*, with public fountains playing
and flags flying (Fig 7). These suggest the architecture of exhibitions and there
are similarities to the Glasgow Exhibition designed by Thomas Tait in 1938,
and to the British Empire Exhibition at Wembley of 1924 (Fig 8). Both had
axial plans with broad streets and consistent white architecture. Abercrombie
did not define the architecture or the materials of the new city but called for a
'coherent architectural treatment', making the analogy to Nash's Regent Street
and referring to 'modern construction techniques' using 'concrete made from
local limestone'.[5] However, Harvey's illustrations show the new civic centre
to be classical (presumably to appeal to councillors), the shops akin to Oxford

Figure 6
*A plan of Delhi drawn by Gavin Stamp based on
Edwin Lutyens's plan for New Delhi (1912).
[Stamp, G 1976 'Indian Summer'.* Architectural
Review *159, 365–72, 366]*

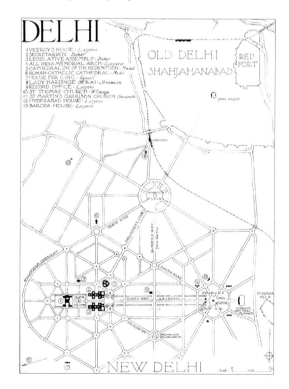

Figure 7
Shopping centre drawn by J D M Harvey from
A Plan for Plymouth.
[Abercrombie and Paton Watson 1943, 74.
Reproduced by permission of the Plymouth and
West Devon Record Office, Ref 1655]

Figure 8
Map of the British Empire Exhibition, 1924.
[© Museum of London, Image No 004171]

Figure 9
The Civic Centre drawn by
J D M Harvey from A Plan for
Plymouth.
[Abercrombie and Paton
Watson 1943, 75. Reproduced
by permission of the Plymouth
and West Devon Record Office,
Ref 1655]

Figure 10
North Cross and the Railway
Hotel drawn by J D M Harvey
from A Plan for Plymouth.
[Abercrombie and Paton
Watson 1943, 70. Reproduced
by permission of the Plymouth
and West Devon Record Office,
Ref 1655]

Circus and the main axis marked by symmetrical pylons like Tait's at Glasgow or, even, Lutyens's Cenotaph in Whitehall (Figs 9 and 10).

In common with many of his contemporaries, Abercrombie despised all things Victorian. The Victorian city with its muddled architecture, unsanitary conditions and mixed uses represented all that was wrong with city design. He used this argument to remove the Victorian houses of the West Hoe (even though they were unscathed), the damaged pier (described as 'the one ugly feature' marring 'a promenade of unequalled historic and natural beauty') and the Guildhall, Prudential Assurance and other Victorian buildings which could have been repaired but which 'interfered' with the *Plan*.[6] The functions of a new city, he argued, must be strictly zoned and he realised that zoning the city would simplify development and help developers, planners and central government (in the shape of the new Ministry of Town & Country Planning) achieve the plan. The tone of the *Plan* is consistently optimistic – there was no doubt in the authors' minds that this proposal, or something very close to it, was going to be realised sooner rather than later and that the rebuilding of Plymouth was going to be symbolic of the rebuilding of a better Britain.

2

Realising the *Plan* 1945–51 and 1951–62 (the city centre)

Plymouth was the only British city to retain its wartime planner and in doing so displayed a political instinct which was to ensure that it remained ahead of all other cities in the reconstruction process. The City Council adopted *A Plan for Plymouth* in September 1944 and its execution was delegated to a politically neutral Reconstruction Committee, chaired initially by Sir Clifford Tozer, the Conservative leader and chairman of Tozer's department store. Lord Astor, who was in poor health, was seconded to the committee and its first act was to appoint Abercrombie as consultant until 1947. Abercrombie's connections and knowledge of the workings of the fledgling Ministry of Town & Country Planning (MTCP, where his former pupils were either staff or advisors) were vital. His reputation was unquestioned – he was knighted in 1945 and received the RIBA's Royal Gold Medal for Architecture in 1946. In 1945, a Labour government was elected on the promise of delivering a 'New Jerusalem' and Plymouth returned three Labour Members of Parliament for the first time. H Moses Medland, MP for Plymouth Drake and vice-chairman of the Reconstruction Committee, struck up a personal friendship with Dame Evelyn Sharp, Deputy Secretary of the MTCP. The new city was exhibited at the House of Commons, ministers were lobbied enthusiastically and the Director of Education, Andrew Scotland, produced an abbreviated version of the *Plan* for local schoolchildren. Plymouth was the first city to complete its public enquiry and the first to place 'declaratory orders' before the MTCP for the compulsory purchase of city centre land. Despite the lack of money and the procrastinations of the bureaucrats at the MTCP and Ministry of Transport, the layout of the new city centre was approved in July 1946 and work began on the new sewers in Raleigh Street in March 1947. King George VI opened the first section of Royal Parade in October, paid for by money diverted from the royal visit.

The practical translation of the *Plan* was left to Paton Watson's department and the city architect, Edgar Catchpole; the compulsory purchases were handled by Colin Campbell, the town clerk, and William Shepherd, the city valuer. The revised plan retained the West Hoe and, within the city centre, more old buildings were kept, including the Odeon (formerly Regent) and Royal cinemas, the *Western Morning News* office, the Methodist church hall and the telephone exchange behind Old Town Street. The main north–south axis, Armada Way, and the cross streets, New George Street, Cornwall Street and Mayflower Street, were narrowed to give more space for the shops. Abercrombie's

The west elevation of the Civic Centre, Armada Way/Royal Parade with Wilts & Dorset Bank (now a bar) 1889 and Derry's Clock Tower 1862, surviving from the Victorian city.
Jellicoe Ballantyne & Coleridge with H J W Stirling, city architect, 1954–61.
[DP086649]

semicircular road layout and most of the narrow 'Bath-like' cross streets disappeared and the spaces between the main streets were filled with simple, doughnut-shaped blocks of outward-facing shops with service courts within. Royal Parade lost its central garden and the Ministry of Transport, which funded trunk roads, specified its width, gradients and roundabouts. The need for space around the telephone exchange meant that Old Town Street swung westwards and Exeter Street (the east side of the gyratory road) was pushed eastwards. The ruined Charles Church, which had been left as a war memorial and which Abercrombie had intended to be part of the 'historic Plymouth' precinct, was now encircled by a busy roundabout. The bus station was tucked under the elevated level of Exeter Street rather than being part of North Hill railway station. Despite the simplification, compromises and the erosion of the symmetry of the *Plan*, the revised plan retained the principles of the precincts, the rigid zoning and the rectilinear geometry of the original (Fig 11).

Abercrombie realised that the city officers would be unable to control the quality and consistency of design that the new city centre demanded and recommended the appointment of an independent consultant architect, William Crabtree. Crabtree had made his reputation in the 1930s with his Peter Jones department store in Chelsea and was an Abercrombie pupil from Liverpool. Crabtree with the city engineer and city architect predetermined the widths and levels of the roads and pavements, the division of every block into separate building plots and the overall height, cornice lines and the sizes of shopfronts of the future buildings. Crabtree seems to have been at odds with the city from the outset and, when his work of vetting the many planning applications became more onerous in 1948, it was agreed that Thomas Tait, the architect of the first new building in the city, Dingles department store, should also become design consultant. Tait was at the end of an illustrious career as the senior partner of Sir John Burnet Tait & Lorne, the most important London firm of the inter-war period, and architect of the Sydney Harbour Bridge, as well as Lloyds Bank in Cornhill and many other important London buildings. He threw himself enthusiastically into his new job and his influence on the form of the city blocks and on the architecture, especially of Royal Parade, was immediate. Tait designed Dingles and, with the commercial architects Alec French of Bristol, offices for Royal Insurance on St Andrew's Cross and for Pearl Assurance on Royal Parade. He thus set the style for the new city. The new buildings were in

Figure 11
The revised layout for the central area of Plymouth.
[Rigby Childs, D and Boyne, D A C A 1952 'Plymouth'.
*Architects' Journal **115**, 716–19, 719]*

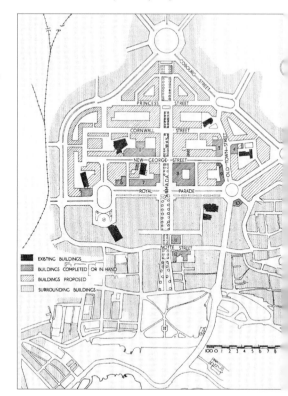

Portland stone, fulfilling Abercrombie's desire for architectural consistency. There was little precedent for this in Plymouth, except that the Naval Memorial and the Royal Cinema were both in Portland stone and there may have been some political expediency in using the quarry that would later rebuild London.

First buildings 1948–53

Within the strict parameters, the design of the buildings was left to individual owners or developers and their architects. Inevitably, at first these were the banks, insurance companies and larger shops that had access to funding and could secure the building licences which allocated scarce materials. Dingles and Pearl Assurance marked the entrance to Armada Way from Royal Parade with squat towers, perhaps suggested by Harvey's pylons which had illustrated the *Plan*, but a typical Tait motif (Fig 12 and 13). About them, the horizontal forms of the buildings were composed. Dingles was the more abstract with strong bands of windows and golden Hamstone divisions incised into the plain stone walls; Pearl was more decorated with flat fluted pilasters and alternating column-and-ball 'mullions' defined by the rhythm of the office windows. These windows, as in almost every building of the city, were carefully proportioned rectangles of slim, elegant metal frames, painted white. By contrast, the shopfronts were cut boldly into the stonework with wide bronze frames. Usually, as at Pearl, the shopfronts had fixed projecting canopies perforated with glass lens lights and holding retractable, vertical canvas blinds, to protect shoppers from the sun and wind. Royal Insurance demonstrated what happened when these design ideas were brought to an office building with no shops (Fig 14). The façade was very plain with a discernable base, middle and cornice of stonework and the first- and second-floor windows were designed together with a metal spandrel panel, suggesting a *piano nobile*. The roots of this architecture are clearly classical. Norwich Union House by the London commercial architects, Donald Hamilton Wakeford & Partners, which turned the corners of Royal Parade, Old Town Street and New George Street, showed how the style was manipulated (Fig 15). Each façade was symmetrical, the continuous base expressed by the canopy and shops, the cornice in a very thin band of stone and the columns between pulled away from the office windows.

Figure 14
*Royal Insurance (now Royal Building),
St Andrew's Cross.*
*Alec F French & Partners in association
with Sir John Burnet Tait & Partners,
1949–53.*
[DP086667]

Figure 15
*Norwich Union House, St Andrew's Cross/
Old Town Street.*
*Donald Hamilton Wakeford & Partners,
1950–2.*
[DP086552]

Figure 16 (left)
Plymouth Co-op (formerly Derrys),
Derry's Cross.
W J Reed, staff architect to Co-operative
Wholesale Society, 1950–2.
[DP086664]

The main façade, facing St Andrew's Cross, was very grand indeed with a huge bronze central window flanked by columns and fluted pilasters. It is reminiscent of the stripped classical architecture of the Paris International Exhibition of 1937. The Co-op, at the west end of Royal Parade, the only shop to occupy a complete city block, illustrates just how liberal Tait and Crabtree's approval of other architects' designs could be. This also expressed its columns externally, but the façade was an abstract, continuous composition of windows and translucent glass blocks and its cornice a continuous balcony, the soffit of which was painted bright yellow (Fig 16). Despite the rules, the new architecture of Plymouth was infinitely variable.

There were occasions when the consultants knew to leave well alone. Barclays Bank headquarters, where Armada Way met Notte Street in the civic precinct, was designed by W Curtis Green, Son & Lloyd of London (Fig 17). Curtis Green was awarded the Royal Gold Medal for Architecture in 1942 and the firm had an established reputation. They produced the most overtly classical building of the new city, a delicate essay in careful proportion and beautiful detailing of polished granite and Portland stone. Unfortunately, the upper two floors of the building were never completed and therefore the bank did not establish the scale intended for the precinct. Elsewhere, planning applications were unaltered for reasons of commercial expediency. For example, the façades of Marks & Spencer by the London firm of Lewis & Hickey

Figure 17 (right)
Barclays Bank, Notte Street/Armada Way.
(altered 2006).
W Curtis Green RA Son & Lloyd, 1949–52 .

were more or less standard for any city. The Plymouth version set a pompous neo-Egyptian façade to Cornwall Street but the scale was about right. A more abstract, so-called 'modular' façade on Old Town Street, based on a 1930s design by Robert Lutyens, Sir Edwin's son, was rather more suitable. Not all national retailers came off so lightly. Burton's on Old Town Street were persuaded to reject their standard pre-war black granite art-deco façade for Portland stone in exchange for permission to use their upper floor as a billiard hall. The design for Boots the Chemist on the corner of New George Street and Old Town Street by their staff architect, Colin St Clair Oakes, was morphed from art deco to something much plainer although the porthole and lozenge-shaped windows from the first designs remained.

The 1950s was the last period when applied art and architecture went hand in hand. Both local and nationally known artists and sculptors decorated the new architecture of Plymouth. There were murals (often based on themes of Drake and the Armada) and sculpture, depicting exotic fruits, for example on Dingles (Fig 18) and the Co-op – or more allegorical, like the figures by William

Figure 18
Relief panel on Dingles department store, Royal Parade. Unknown sculptor, 1951. [DP086627]

Figure 19
Figures on west elevation of Barclays Bank, Armada Way. William McMillan, 1952. [DP086669 & DP086670]

McMillan on Barclays Bank (Fig 19) and the Naval Memorial on the Hoe, and the reliefs by Bainbridge Copnall (who had worked on the RIBA Headquarters in London in the 1930s) on Marks & Spencer (Fig 20). Later, the major public buildings of the city, the Pannier Market, the Guildhall, the Crown Courts and Civic Centre gave the opportunity for incorporating more abstract public art.

Most important of all, the care taken to compose the building façades was carried through into the composition of the overall city. The idea of the Beaux-Arts axis was applied to all the major streets as well as the symmetrical spaces up Armada Way. Thus the axis of Royal Parade terminated on the portico of the National Provincial Bank at St Andrew's Cross and on the stair and lift tower of the Gas Board at Derry's Cross; Eastlake Street was symmetrical to the Old Town Street façade of Marks & Spencer and New George Street terminated exactly on the flagpole which marked the centre of the Westminster Bank on Old Town Street. Courtenay Street and Bedford Way were aligned precisely to façades on the north side of New George Street and the Pannier Market was symmetrical to Cornwall Street and New George Street and aligned symmetrically to the space of Frankfort Gate. These compositions may also have been used to justify the shift of Exeter Street, for it lined exactly with the spire of the Charles Church and the tower of St Andrew's, which had not been suggested in the original *Plan*. There were some more subtle asymmetrical compositions. For example, the west part of New George Street was a composition of major and minor rhythms between the larger shops like Woolworth's and the rows of smaller shops which filled the gaps in between to a consistent cornice height (Fig 21). Of these, Nos 70–8 New George Street was the only building designed in detail by Crabtree, although it was executed by other architects. In the grid plan, the corner buildings were very important and were usually used to establish the scale of the adjacent streets. These corners were rarely symmetrical and Plymouth had a huge variety of different corner designs, including splays, concave and convex curves, re-entrant angles, cantilevers and plain right angles.

Not all the buildings were in Portland stone. This too may be explained by the idea of compositional balance across the city. The old *Western Morning News* building on New George Street, which was red-brick neo-Georgian with a pitched tiled roof, justified further red-brick buildings on the eastern part of New George Street, across Armada Way. The first was Ellis Somake's Dolcis

Figure 20
Sculpted panel of a mermaid on Marks & Spencer, Old Town Street. This is set high up within the modular façade, originally facing down Eastlake Street. E Bainbridge Copnall, 1952.
[DP086707]

shoe shop that was part of the Dingles' block and designed and built at the same time (Fig 22). Somake framed the whole three storeys in narrow 'Dutch' red brick which enclosed a huge aluminium-framed curtain-wall window. At night, the stylish interior with bright coloured panels, 'tulip' pendant lights and spindly modern furniture was visible from the street. It gave Plymothians their first glimpse of the contemporary modern style of the Festival of Britain which was very different from Tait's architecture of mass. The idea of 'balancing' brick across the city occurred on the north–south axis too. Below Notte Street, most notably in Messrs Joseph's Navy, Army and Air Force Institutes (NAAFI) Services' Club, and in Cornwall Street and Armada Way north from Mayflower Street, buildings were in plain red brick with details only in stone. By far the most sophisticated was the NAAFI (Fig 23). Its elevations were based on the famous City Hall at Norwich by C H James & S R

Figure 21
New George Street (left to right): Littlewoods, Nos 82–6 New George Street (replacing the Odeon Cinema, now T J Hughes); Nos 70–8 New George Street; Woolworth's, Nos 66–8 New George Street; Nos 52–64 New George Street; Jacksons, 50 New George Street/Armada Way. Littlewoods Stores staff architect, 1963; William Crabtree and other architects, 1949; W A Draysey, Woolworth's staff architect, 1949–51; W H Watkins & Partners, 1950; N Martin, Jacksons staff architect, 1950–5.

Figure 22
Dolcis shoe shop (now three separate shops), New George Street.
Ellis E Somake, staff architect to Upsons Ltd, 1949–51.
[DP086810]

Figure 23
NAAFI (Navy, Army and Air Force Institutes) Services' Club (now the Hoe Centre), Armada Way/Notte Street (demolished 2010).
Messrs Joseph, 1949–51.
[DP086632]

Pierce of 1932–8 which, in turn, was based on Swedish precedents. The fluted columns on the NAAFI staircase window came from Stockholm Town Hall, designed by Ragnar Östberg in 1903–23, and the Dutch architect, Willem Dudok, who won the Royal Gold Medal in 1935, influenced its handsome brickwork details and tower.

Separate buildings – churches, banks, the Pannier Market and Athenaeum 1953–62

No other building symbolised the rebuilding of Plymouth more than the restoration of St Andrew's Church. There was never any debate about leaving the ruins as a war memorial as there was for the Charles Church or, for example, Coventry Cathedral. The architect was Frederick Etchells, known as the translator of the works of the Swiss modernist architect, Le Corbusier, but whose practice specialised in church repair. Etchells restored the exterior more or less to its medieval appearance. Inside, the new roof vaults over the nave and aisles were thin-cast concrete shells, a very modern construction, but Etchells camouflaged them with appliqué oak ribs and false oak wall plates. All the interior fittings were designed by Etchells in oak, copying historic patterns. This made more surprising, therefore, the commissioning of John Piper and Patrick Reyntiens to design new stained glass windows. Piper and Reyntiens had worked on many new churches including Coventry Cathedral and Piper was probably the most famous modern British artist of the time. The five windows at the east end of the church, installed into the Gothic tracery in 1965, were highly abstract and brightly coloured and a very effective foil to Etchells's rather academic and monotone interior (Fig 24). The west window of 1958, a representation of the Instruments of the Passion and a memorial to Lord Astor, was more figurative as befitted its dedication.

New churches were grouped together, south of the civic precinct in Notte Street and south of St Andrew's and the old synagogue, demonstrating that the

Figure 24
Rebuilding of St Andrew's Church, Royal Parade, looking east. Windows by John Piper and Patrick Reyntiens, 1965.
Frederick Etchells, 1945–57.

Figure 25 (above left)
Unitarian Church, Notte Street.
Louis de Soissons RA & Partners, 1955–8.
[DP069420]

Figure 26 (above right)
Baptist Church, Catherine Street.
Louis de Soissons RA & Partners (Louis de Soissons, Peacock, Hodges, Robertson & Fraser), 1956–9.
[DP069435]

zoning rules applied to all building types. Only the Methodist church was remote, placed at the west end of Foulston's Crescent and designed in brick by the Welsh architect and Royal Gold medallist of 1939, Sir Percy Thomas (*see* Fig 76). It seems that the churches were anxious to reassert their position in post-war society by commissioning significant architects and artists. The Unitarian and Baptist churches were by Louis de Soissons, the architect and planner of Welwyn Garden City (Figs 25 and 26). De Soissons was French Canadian and had trained at the École des Beaux-Arts in Paris but was an admirer of the architecture of New England and, perhaps fittingly, he used these colonial motifs in Plymouth. Both churches have pitched roofs, classical pediments and slender, decorated copper spires. Although their budgets were modest, both were beautifully and sparingly detailed. The interior of the

Figure 27
Baptist Church, Catherine Street. Interior looking north with Hans
Feibusch's mural, The Baptism of Christ, *1959, above the communion table.*
Louis de Soissons RA & Partners (Louis de Soissons, Peacock, Hodges,
Robertson & Fraser), 1956–9.
[DP086817]

Baptist church was exceptionally fine with limed oak pews and pulpit, 'tulip' light fittings and a huge mural of the *Baptism of Christ* by Hans Feibusch, the émigré German painter (Fig 27). The Catholic church of 1961–2 was placed on Armada Way south of Notte Street and therefore it was in brick, and its campanile was intended to balance the tower of the NAAFI across the axis (Fig 28). This was the last work of Sir Giles Gilbert Scott who had devoted his life to the building of Liverpool Anglican Cathedral, although it had much in common with the many smaller churches that his office had designed from 1906. The brickwork, campanile, Roman-tiled roof and Gothic windows gave it a curiously Italianate character in miniature.

There was a problem of the scale for these churches for it was only the department stores and the banks that could realise the city scale that Abercrombie's streets demanded. The headquarters of the National Provincial Bank by the bank's architect, B C Sherren, was in Portland stone but a huge

Figure 28
Roman Catholic Church of Christ the King,
Armada Way/Notte Street.
Sir Giles Gilbert Scott, Son & Partner, 1960–2.
[DP086444]

Figure 29
National Provincial Bank (now RBS),
St Andrew's Cross.
B C Sherren, staff architect to National
Provincial Bank, 1955–8.
[DP086531]

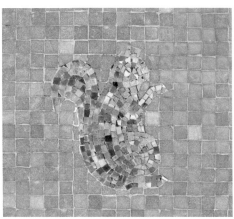

Figure 30
Detail of mosaic cladding on the west
elevation showing a squirrel motif.
[DP086524]

Figure 31
Detail of the lantern that marks the
axis of Royal Parade.
[DP086526]

Figure 32
Lloyds Bank and Popham's department store,
Royal Parade.
Easton & Robertson, 1954–8.
[DP086621]

Figure 33
Sculpture of sea horses by Amyas Munday, 1958.
[DP086623]

stripped classical portico in Devon granite faced Royal Parade (Fig 29). The walls of the public entrance behind it were faced in Mediterranean-blue and lilac glass mosaic studded with gold motifs of fish, anchors, castles and squirrels taken from the bank's coat of arms (Fig 30). It was especially impressive at night when it was lit from behind the columns. Bronze doors framed in white marble led to a sumptuous treble-height banking hall, paved in travertine marble with teak, padouk and bronze fittings. The roof was curved copper, crowned with an illuminated green glass lantern holding a clock which marked the axis (Fig 31). Lloyds Bank on Royal Parade by Easton & Robertson was less opulent but also based on classical composition (Fig 32). Its scale was increased by incorporating Popham's department store, hence the twin entrances. J Murray Easton and Howard Robertson were both Royal Gold medallists (in 1955 and 1949 respectively) and Robertson in his *Principles of Architectural Composition* (1924) had admired the commercial classical architecture of America. Lloyds followed these examples by emphasising vertical proportions with strongly expressed stone columns finishing on a projecting cornice. The three-storey curtain wall between the columns was of dark teak, unique to Plymouth, and a local sculptor Amyas Munday, added sea horses and dolphins high up on the attic storey (Fig 33).

The same problem of scale existed for the Pannier Market, which was placed away from the department stores at the west end of the city centre and was essentially a single-storey building. It was designed by Walls & Pearn, the only major building in the city centre by local architects (Figs 34 and 35). Here was the opportunity to reject classical composition and, together with their structural engineer Albin Chronowicz, they produced a cathedral-like hall 40ft (12.2m) high with seven great concrete portal frames spanning 150ft (45.7m) and thin concrete shell vaults between forming rooflights. It was in a modern tradition of raw concrete structures which had their sources in inter-war

Figure 34
Pannier Market, New George Street/ Frankfort Gate/Cornwall Street (altered c 1999).
Walls & Pearn, 1956–9.

Figure 35
The concrete vaults and northlights
(rooflights facing north) over the market hall
in the Pannier Market.
Walls & Pearn, 1956–9.

Fig 36
Mural in south porch of the Pannier Market
by David Weeks, 1959.
[DP086574]

Germany. Examples came to prominence in the austere post-war years, most notably with the Brynmawr Rubber Factory of 1948–52 in Wales and examples from France, Italy and South America had inspired readers of the *Architectural Review* since the war. Like Brynmawr, the Pannier Market was also decorated – painted bright blue and yellow and with murals by the sculptor David Weeks in the porches (Fig 36). The undulating canopies on the south and north sides were a reference to Jane Drew's Thameside Restaurant at the Festival of Britain and another was to be found in Walls & Pearn's Athenaeum (1958–61) on Derry's Cross (Fig 37). Its façade was a delicate miniaturisation of the Royal Festival Hall, proving, once again, how important 'Festival' architecture was to the provinces. The Athenaeum was structurally innovative too, using a revolutionary steel space frame to span the auditorium. The Pannier Market

Figure 37
Athenaeum, Derry's Cross. The symmetrical north elevation facing Derry's Cross and axial to Raleigh Street.
Walls & Pearn, 1958–61
[DP086703]

and Athenaeum were symbolically significant, for they show a city confident enough by the late 1950s to replace the cultural and social institutions that had been lost in the war with original and optimistic *modern* buildings that expressed a new spirit for a new city.

Completing the city centre – shops, old buildings and landscape 1953–62

Figure 38
Nos 15-17 New George Street (left) and
No 19 New George Street (centre).
Red brick and framed-out windows.
A J Ardin with Edgar Catchpole, city architect,
1955-6; Edward Narracott with Edgar Catchpole,
city architect, 1954-5.

Crabtree and Tait's contracts were not renewed after 1952 and Catchpole was the sole coordinating architect for the city centre until his retirement in 1954. His influence may be seen in the consistent architecture produced on the west side of Derry's Cross, on the south side of Cornwall Street from Armada Way to Marks & Spencer, and on a set of three façades at the east end of New George Street. These latter were red brick with Portland stone trimmings and flank walls, based loosely on Ralph Tubbs's Indian Students' Hostel in Fitzroy Square, London, which had been extensively published in the architectural press (Fig 38). A new city architect, Hector Stirling, was appointed in 1951. Under his influence the materials, if not the style, of the city centre buildings changed. There was more brick and more reconstructed Portland stone, both cheaper than real stone, and there were more infill panels of different materials such as Westmorland slate, concrete aggregate, coloured tiles and coloured aluminium, often dark green. Gradually, the ubiquitous steel windows gave way to aluminium curtain walls or timber frames. As an age of austerity changed to an age of affluence, architects were impatient to use the variety of materials that the building industry could now offer them. Paton Watson retired in 1958 and the controls that he had devised were relaxed. Strict regulation that was unquestioned in the early 1950s was less acceptable to a population of traders and developers who had 'never had it so good' in the relatively affluent late 1950s. Perversely, less money was spent on buildings as private wealth increased. Developers realised that cheaply built shops would let easily and shopkeepers realised that, as tenants not owner-occupiers, investment in expensive buildings and shop fitting was unnecessary. Most of the national retailers, the banks and department stores had been fitted into the southern end of the shopping precinct and only the smaller, local shops were available for the

Figure 39
Flats and shops, Frankfort Gate.
H J W Stirling, city architect
with John Laing Construction,
1955–7.
[DP086807]

northern part. The city stuck rigidly to the original zoning and consistently refused permission for flats or offices over shops and therefore it was impossible to produce buildings of the four or five storeys that the streets were designed to receive. The quality and scale of much of Cornwall Street, Mayflower Street and especially the western area along Union Street and Western Approach were significantly lower than the earlier parts of the *Plan*. However, the problem forced the city to introduce housing within the ring road – a major departure – and modest four-storey brick-faced flats were introduced at Frankfort Gate, designed by Stirling using the 'Easiform' prefabricated building system (Fig 39).

Frankfort Gate introduced the only formal public square of the *Plan*, paved and simply planted with plane trees. Neither Abercrombie nor the city thereafter consulted a landscape architect; the city engineer's department carried out all the design of the streets, pavements and planting. The road kerbstones were granite, reused from the old city and, where new kerbs were required, for paving or gardens, they were in boldly moulded concrete. The most successful planting was the avenue of lime trees along the south side of Royal Parade which showed how powerful Abercrombie's idea of a boulevard for the whole gyratory road would have been. At the top of Armada Way, above

Figure 40
Braille Garden, Armada Way. This photo shows the original planting of cockspur thorn trees with the brick façade of the YMCA behind.
H J W Stirling, city architect and city engineer's department, Braille Garden, 1958. Alec French & Partners, YMCA, 1953–8
[DP086877]

Mayflower Street where the 200ft (61m) width had been retained, Stirling and Paton Watson created an ornamental 'Braille Garden' with aromatic plants and an enormous basin made and decorated with stones from old buildings (Fig 40). This was intended to balance a huge waterfall on the slope up to the Hoe, south of Notte Street, which had been drawn in the *Plan*. The space immediately below the Braille Garden was a 'collegiate' lawn and the three

spaces between the cross streets in the shopping precinct were also lawns, surrounded on both sides by parked cars. The maintenance of a clear vista from North Cross to the Hoe was paramount. From 1951, Stirling began to develop ideas for a 'Great Square' in the civic precinct, south of Royal Parade. This idea was reinforced by the decision to retain and restore the Guildhall and to turn its entrance from the north side to the west to address the new space. The civic offices would be a tower to balance the tower of the Guildhall and the council chamber would face a concert hall across the square.

Guildhall and Civic Centre 1951–62

Stirling's restoration of the Guildhall was far less doctrinaire or archaeological than that by Etchells for St Andrew's. Although he restored the main pitched roof and repaired the gothic windows, the low front roofs were flat and all the new elements were distinctly modern (Fig 41). This was proclaimed in the new entrance with its undulating, coffered canopy but the drama was reserved for the lobbies and Great Hall where he created one of the best and richest interiors of the 1950s. The floors of the lobby were white terrazzo with white marble walls, mahogany joinery and bronze doors; the stair in white marble with a quilted blue-leather handrail studded in bronze; the Great Hall was panelled in Cuban mahogany. The curved plaster ceiling was decorated with the *Labours of Hercules* by David Weeks and the windows contained painted glass by F H Coventry depicting scenes from local history. Three huge chandeliers hung from the ceiling, symbolising the three towns of Plymouth (Fig 42).

At the same time, Stirling was developing the designs for the concert hall and Civic Centre. Both projects ran into difficulties. The city decided that the concert hall was too expensive and the site was given to the Crown Courts, funded by the Lord Chancellor. Stirling completed the designs of the Civic Centre and courts but the city would not give him the staff for the technical drawings and the responsibility for completing them was handed to the London firm of Jellicoe Ballantyne & Coleridge. Geoffrey Jellicoe is known today principally as a landscape architect, but he was part of the architectural establishment and a member of the Royal Fine Art Commission that had

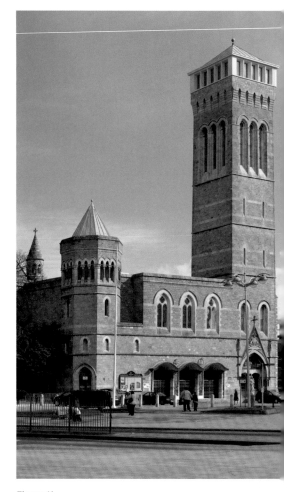

Figure 41
Guildhall, Armada Way. New main entrance
facing the Great Square.
H J W Stirling, city architect, 1953–9
[DP086639]

Figure 42
Guildhall, Armada Way. Interior showing David
Weeks's Labours of Hercules, *the Gobelin tapestry*
of the Miraculous Draught of Fishes *and the three*
chandeliers.
H J W Stirling, city architect, 1953–9

approved Stirling's design for the Civic Centre. It was based on Lever House in New York, the office building by Skidmore Owings & Merrill which had rocked the architectural world in the early 1950s. A 12-storey tower parallel to Armada Way sat on a two-storey podium that conformed to the orthogonal grid of the city (Fig 43). Stirling had intended the tower to be clad in glass like Lever House, but Jellicoe and Ballantyne revised it to two-tone concrete panels cast from Devon granite aggregate and faced the base in riven Delabole slate to

Figure 43
Civic Centre, Armada Way.
Jellicoe Ballantyne & Coleridge with
H J W Stirling, city architect, 1954–61.
Geoffrey Jellicoe, landscape architect,
Great Square, 1961.
[DP069409]

Figure 44
Interior of council chamber with Hans Tisdall
murals, Civic Centre, Armada Way.
Jellicoe Ballantyne & Coleridge with H J W Stirling,
city architect, 1954–61.
[DP034877]

give it a more local context. Inside, walls were faced in dark Ashburton marble and plain timber panels, reflecting the more international style of the late 1950s that Ballantyne had seen in Denmark in the work of Arne Jacobsen. The council suite was sumptuously decorated with etched glass by John Hutton (who had worked on Coventry Cathedral) and a mural by Mary Adshead, while the walls of the chamber were covered in decorated fabric and painted panels on heraldic themes by Hans Tisdall, another émigré German artist (Fig 44). The council suite was connected to the podium with bridges, forming a courtyard which Jellicoe filled with a reflecting pool as part of the overall landscape of the Great Square. Here he retained the trees from the old Westwell Street gardens and around them built circular seats, another broad pool, swirling paving and raised flower beds. It showed how good the spaces of Armada Way could be in experienced hands. The Civic Centre and Great Square were the finale of the plan for Plymouth. The achievement was proudly celebrated by the public restaurant and terrace on the top floor of the Civic Centre tower from which the grateful citizens could admire their new city. The Civic Centre embodies, as no other building, the hopes and aspirations of a newly confident City Council and serves as a striking testimony to the spirit which guided the reconstruction.

3

Housing and the suburbs

Ideas for new housing and the planning of the suburbs were presented statistically rather than visually in *A Plan for Plymouth*. The statistics were daunting. Abercrombie argued that the surviving city centre housing was far too dense and proposed a maximum density of 100 persons per acre (it was 253 in the central Vintry ward), reducing to 50 persons per acre in the existing suburbs and to 25 persons per acre for the new suburbs. Adding together the replacement of war- damaged houses, the predicted increase in post-war families and the known pre-war housing shortage, housing displaced by the expansion of the Devonport dockyard and the re-zoning of Stonehouse as an industrial area, and the replacement of slums, Abercrombie calculated that some 33,000 new houses were required. Almost 64,000 people needed 'redistribution' of whom only 24,000 could be placed within the existing city boundary, leaving 40,000 to be housed beyond in new suburbs. In describing these suburbs, Abercrombie was much influenced by Lewis Mumford, the American historian and theorist, whose *The Culture of Cities* had been published in 1938. Mumford stressed the need to build communities centred on schools and cultural activities, safe from the motor car, affording personal privacy and communal enjoyment of open space.

> There is not a village or housing Estate that is well planned, unless it has made provision for places of withdrawal – solitary walks, devious woodland paths – no less than places where people can gather together in groups for social communion.[7]

Thus Abercrombie's vision was of new communities of a finite size surrounded by parkland or woodland, forming a natural extension of the city parks or of the countryside on which they would be built. The smallest group was to be the 'residential unit' around a nursery school. A number of residential units would make up a 'neighbourhood group', based around an elementary school, with no through road traffic and a population of between 6,000 and 10,000. At its heart would be a 'neighbourhood centre' consisting of a church, library, swimming bath, cinema, shops, laundry, child welfare and other clinics and a community building where 'citizens amuse themselves rather than listen to performances by experts'.[8] Four or five neighbourhood centres would combine to support bigger community buildings without diluting the importance of the

Aerial view of Ham. Dryburgh Crescent and Jedburgh Crescent enclosing South Trelawny Primary School (demolished 2010) with Ham Green (top right), all completed before 1952. [NMR/26405/002]

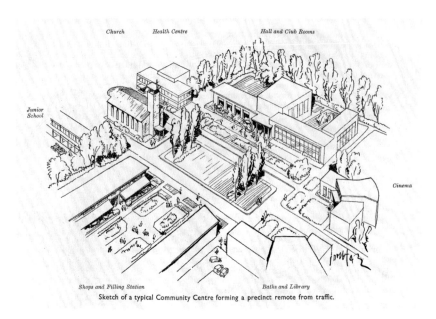

Sketch of a typical Community Centre forming a precinct remote from traffic.

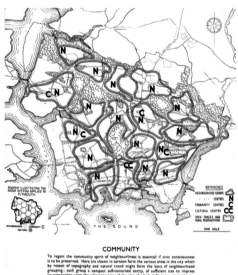

city centre, fitting conveniently into Mumford's idea of the 'polycentric' city. The *Plan* did illustrate a typical community centre – an orthogonal arrangement of single and two-storey buildings around a green – and a plan of the city showing the neighbourhood groups, either formed from existing housing within the old city or new estates, stretching northwards beyond the A38 Parkway and separated by green belts (Figs 45 and 46). Behind the mathematical, statistical approach to the problem, is revealed a strong sense of Abercrombie's social democratic ideals that exactly captured the spirit of the times.

Figure 45 (above left)
Typical community centre drawn by
J D M Harvey from A Plan for Plymouth.
[Abercrombie and Paton Watson 1943, 84.
Reproduced by permission of the Plymouth
and West Devon Record Office, Ref 1655]

Figure 46 (above right)
Community – a diagram of the neighbourhood
grouping from A Plan for Plymouth.
[Abercrombie and Paton Watson 1943, 78.
Reproduced by permission of the Plymouth
and West Devon Record Office, Ref 1655]

Housing in the new suburbs

The new suburbs – Ernesettle, Ham and Pennycross, Honicknowle, Whitleigh, Efford and Southway – were built on the farms and farmland after which they were named – a green, undulating countryside of woods, fields and hedgerows. The villages of King's Tamerton and Tamerton Foliot were incorporated,

Crownhill became one of the neighbourhood centres and outlying cottages, for example at Honicknowle, were integrated into the new layouts (Fig 47). The design of the new suburbs fell to Edgar Catchpole and the city engineer's department and their delivery to the city housing department as agents of the Ministry of Housing and Aneurin Bevan's vision of the 'New Jerusalem'. This was council housing to a standard and scale never before contemplated. Private development was relegated to one small area in Hartley Vale and Eggbuckland and east of the River Plym in Plympton and Plymstock. The layouts of the suburbs followed a standard pattern. The schools at the centre of

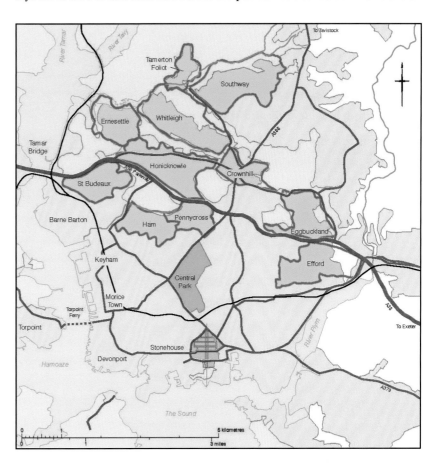

Figure 47
A map showing Plymouth's suburbs.

Figure 48
Aerial view of Ernesettle centred on Ernesettle Green with Tamerton Lake and Budshead Creek in the foreground.
[NMR/26404/022]

the community were built on the hilltops where the ground was flattest for playgrounds and sports fields. Around them, the houses were built along the contours in long ribbons of two-storey, semi-detached or short terraces more or less parallel to the roads with footpaths connecting them. Each community was surrounded by 'arcadian' wooded valleys, open for recreation as Abercrombie had intended, and there was generous provision of more communal greenspace amongst the houses in the form of small greens or much larger 'village greens' as at Ernesettle (circular), Honicknowle (square) or Whitleigh and Ham (both triangular) (Fig 48). The community buildings – shops, churches and public houses – were placed loosely around these village greens and only the more rectilinear centre at Efford slightly resembled the illustration of the neighbourhood centre in the *Plan*. Where possible, existing trees and hedgerows were retained but, otherwise, the city engineer designed new planting which formed grand avenues or more picturesque clumps of ornamental trees. Because of the contours, the effect was one of informality but there were axial arrangements – such as Whitleigh Way and its bridge (designed by Drake & Lasdun after a competition in 1950) or the avenues of Biggin Hill at Ernesettle, Blandford Road at Efford and Careswell Avenue at Ham (Fig 49). All the houses faced roads, with small front gardens and long, private back gardens intended for growing vegetables.

Figure 49
Laing Easiform houses set in a formal landscape, Careswell Avenue, Ham, c 1950.

There were precedents for this type of planning in the inter-war estates at St Budeaux and at Mount Gould which are mentioned in the *Plan*. However, the principal influence was from the layouts at Letchworth (from 1904) and Welwyn Garden City (from 1920) in Hertfordshire which had given built form to Ebenezer Howard's vision of the Garden City set out in his *Tomorrow: A Peaceful Path to Real Reform* of 1898. Abercrombie had designed Dormanstown, near Redcar, North Yorkshire, in a similar vein using Adshead & Ramsey, who had worked at Letchworth, as architects for the houses. The London County Council had demonstrated that such layouts were suitable for council housing at a large scale in the St Helier estate at Morden, Surrey, and the Becontree estate near Barking, Essex, in the 1920s. Both Abercrombie's idea of restricting the size of the separate communities and Catchpole's introduction of large village greens humanised the appearance of the Plymouth estates, especially when the architecture was likely to be more modest than even the plain red brick of the LCC. The idea of the new communities being 'villages' is not mentioned in the *Plan* but it is a recurring theme in post-war planning, for example in Thomas Sharp's *The Anatomy of the Village*, a best-seller in 1946. Village greens formed a fundamental theme in the 'Reilly Plan' for Birkenhead proposed in 1944 by Sir Charles Reilly, the former head of the Liverpool School of Architecture and colleague of Abercrombie. The village and its green were powerful symbols of Englishness and therefore something worth fighting for and an ideal to be achieved in peacetime.

Since there were severe shortages of skilled labour and materials, Plymouth, like other local authorities, turned to prefabricated building systems to deliver the houses at the speed and cost required. There were three main types. Laing's 'Easiform' was a system of *in situ* concrete cast into standard forms, pebble-dashed and given a traditional pitched tiled roof and tile-hung bay windows (Fig 50). Selleck Nicolls & Co of St Austell produced the 'Cornish Unit' made from precast concrete posts and planks (using waste from china clay mining) with a timber-framed upper floor clad in tiles in a Mansard form (Fig 51). The British Iron & Steel Federation produced the BISF Type A house, designed by the architect Frederick Gibberd and engineer Donovan Lee, its steel frame clad on the ground floor with blocks, bricks or render and on the first floor with corrugated steel sheeting which was also

Figure 50
Laing Easiform houses at Uxbridge Drive,
Ernesettle, c *1950.*

Figure 51
Cornish Units at Hornchurch Road, Ernesettle,
1952.
[DP086897]

Figure 52
BISF Type A houses at Dryburgh Crescent,
Ham, c 1949.
[DP086750]

Figure 53
A pair of semi-detached houses marking a corner
at West Malling Avenue/Tangmere Avenue,
Ernesettle. Characteristic door surrounds and
circular window.
Louis de Soissons RA & Partners, c 1950.

used on the pitched roofs (Fig 52). All the houses had thin steel windows and the only decorative element was in their porches, made from steel tube supporting thin steel canopies or in shaped cast concrete. The formation of a level platform cut into the steep contours for the prefabricated houses often resulted in precipitous front steps or back gardens. To overcome this problem and to provide four-bedroomed houses, the city commissioned a series of standard designs from Louis de Soissons, which could be better adapted to specific sloping sites and to mark corners. These were traditionally built with wooden windows and the elevations were more varied than the prefabricated houses with different porches (framed with classical mouldings and keystones) and window patterns. Examples were built at Pennycross, Ham and Ernesettle (Fig 53).

The houses came complete with bathrooms, fitted kitchens, heating and hot water which were a marked and welcome contrast to the temporary housing, slums or cramped shared accommodation that most of the tenants had left behind. Families were often moved in before the houses or the streets and pavements were completed. Judging from published reminiscences, the new communities quickly developed a communal spirit – united in their new lives and in their constant battles against the City Council to complete the building work and provide the amenities that had been promised. A resident of Ernesettle recalled: 'Hot running water, indoor toilet and bath – sheer luxury, no more filling the old zinc bath by the fire once a week. There were no pavements outside, only mud paths, but who cared [the children] could now have a bath when they felt like it – every day – sometimes twice a day.'[9] While parents fretted about the lack of shops and street lighting, the distance to schools, the inadequate public transport and the remoteness from the city centre, the new suburbs became an idyll for the children, who could play in seemingly endless building sites and newly discovered countryside.

> The estate was a marvellous place to grow up. We had all the basic ingredients – lots of open space, woods, parks and of course the creek… Summer days were spent climbing trees, making dens in the woods or playing at the waters edge. Picnics which consisted of spam sandwiches, a packet of crisps and if you didn't have lemonade, a bag of sherbet mixed with a bottle of water, tasted better than any Coke… .[10]

> A small stream ran along the valley there, a large area of grass led from Bodmin Road onto it. It was paradise for the children, who came from many parts of the estate to collect blackberries. Some filled jam-jars with tadpoles, or other water creatures, with which to decorate the kitchen shelves at home.[11]

The city architects under Hector Stirling also designed special housing for sites where the system buildings were thought unsuitable. These were in the centre of Tamerton Foliot and Paton Watson Quadrate (named for Paton Watson's retirement in 1958), below the Citadel in the Barbican, where new buildings were juxtaposed with the old (Fig 54). Here Stirling used a 'conservation' style of varied tiled pitched roofs, stone and tile-hung walls and calculatedly picturesque arches and alleyways surely influenced by the 'townscape' of the *Architectural Review*, drawn so seductively by Gordon Cullen through the 1950s. Other blocks of flats within the city showed that Stirling's department was open to all new influences. On Woolster Street (now Vauxhall Street) in the Barbican they designed four-storey flats with 'Scandinavian'

Figure 54
Housing at Paton Watson Quadrate, Barbican.
H J W Stirling, city architect, 1958.
[DP086735_1]

Figure 55
Housing at Cecil Street, Stonehouse.
H J W Stirling, city architect, 1954.
[DP086747]

Figure 56
Sutton Dwellings Trust housing at Miles Mitchell
Village, Miles Mitchell Avenue/Bickleigh Close,
Eggbuckland.
Louis de Soissons, Peacock, Hodges, Robertson &
Fraser, 1958.
[DP086891]

Figure 57
The Lawns, Crownhill.
Marshman Warren & Taylor, 1966.
[DP087285]

mono-pitched roofs with exposed rafters and elevations hung with Cornish slates. Through the city – on Notte Street, in Cecil Street, Stonehouse (1954) and in Devonport – the department built flats on a standard star-shaped plan borrowed from the Gröndal Estate in Stockholm. This had been presented as an ideal by the architectural press through the late 1940s, but only its form and not its verdant communal landscape was transferred (Fig 55). Private housing did not challenge the pre-war pattern of detached villas and estate roads. However, private housing trusts were willing to experiment. At Mitchell Avenue, Eggbuckland, Louis de Soissons's office designed a delightful group of retirement houses for the Sutton Trust (1958) (Fig 56). This was a village within the suburbs, complete with a community hall and clock tower and groups of terraced bungalows and two-storey flats picturesquely enclosing small village greens. At a more urban scale, Marshman Warren & Taylor of Exeter designed The Lawns at Crownhill for the St Aubyn Trust (1966) (Fig 57). Terraced houses with flat and mono-pitched roofs and plain white walls were grouped around landscaped courtyards, demonstrating that greater urban densities need not compromise privacy or accessibility.

Community buildings

The city architects designed a few free-standing blocks of flats in the suburbs, for example at Terra Nova Green, Milehouse and on the green at Ham, but usually the flats were built over parades of shops. These were to a standard, somewhat utilitarian pattern of four storeys with rear deck access. There were examples at Ernesettle, Ham, Whitleigh and Efford but the most sophisticated was the block facing the green at Honicknowle with a covered columned arcade perforated with circular skylights and maisonettes above (Fig 58). The building of the community facilities, imagined by Abercrombie and included on Catchpole's early site plans, lagged well behind the production of the houses and sometimes never appeared. However, old people's homes designed by Stirling were built opposite the greens at Ernesettle (1954–5) and Whitleigh. The home at Ernesettle was in two mono-pitched blocks finished with coloured render, limestone and timber boarding, demonstrating again how Stirling brought a more humane vocabulary to the city architect's repertoire (Fig 59). Sites were also found for public houses. There were two in Ernesettle, two in Whitleigh and one in Ham. The best of these – the Tiger in Whitleigh and the

Figure 58
Shops and flats at The Green, Honicknowle. Edgar Catchpole, city architect, commenced
c *1952.*

Figure 59
Lakeside Residential Home, Ernesettle Green, Ernesettle. H J W Stirling, city architect, 1954–5.

Figure 60
Lion & Column public house, Ham Green, Ham (demolished 2010).
Louis de Soissons, Peacock, Hodges, Robertson & Fraser, 1957.
[DP086756]

Lion & Column (1957) in Ham – were designed by Louis de Soissons with characteristic pitched roofs and bay windows, the Lion & Column with a Roman clay-tile roof and cedar shingle cladding (Fig 60 and *see* Fig 92). Two very small clinics were built at Ham and Honicknowle, libraries were incorporated into the shops rather than being free-standing buildings, the community centre at Ham was fitted into the converted outbuildings of Ham House and that at Whitleigh did not appear until 1980 and only then by public subscription. The swimming baths and cinemas were forgotten.

By contrast, one of the great successes of the new suburbs was the schools which were built almost as the new population arrived. The design of these, primary and secondary, was shared out between the city architect and Louis de Soissons. The city architect used a standard steel-framed structure forming long, narrow blocks of single-loaded corridors serving classrooms. These were composed into linear, cross, U-, or H-shaped plans with the assembly halls at the centre and the wings making courtyards. The classroom wings were usually of two storeys with flat roofs and long ribbon windows below continuous projecting sunshades in cast concrete. These, the white rendered finish and the asymmetrical compositions gave them a powerful modernist flavour that recalled France, Holland or Germany in the 1930s. Examples, all

Figure 61
Plymview Primary
School, Blandford Road,
Efford.
Edgar Catchpole, city
architect, 1949.
[DP088599]

Figure 62
Knowle Primary School,
Ringmore Way, Whitleigh.
Louis de Soissons &
Partners, 1952.
[DP086896]

Figure 63
West Park Infants School, Wanstead Grove,
Honicknowle.
Louis de Soissons RA & Partners, c 1949.
[DP086765]

built before 1952, included Plymview Primary at Efford (Fig 61), South Trelawny Primary at Ham, Chaucer Primary at Honicknowle and Mill Ford Secondary at Ernesettle, which, uniquely, introduced rubble stonework on its flank walls. The de Soissons office was more willing to experiment, perhaps drawing on a wider experience of school design in other counties, especially from progressive Hertfordshire. The primary school at Ernesettle, for example, used paired classrooms in a stepped plan, each block expressed under a separate pitched roof. Knowle Primary was built into the Palmerston fort with a stepped section and the classrooms under a continuous mono-pitched roof, balancing the natural light (Fig 62). Honicknowle Secondary (1951) was formed around two internal courtyards with a grand entrance under a symmetrical pitched roof and West Park Infants at Honicknowle (1949) took this idea further with an almost classical entrance through a colonnade (Fig 63). De Soissons was experimental with materials too, as on his public houses, using stonework and coloured render externally and coloured terrazzo and timber panelling for internal decorative effect. Whitleigh Primary (1956) and Knowle Primary had especially handsome assembly halls with curved plaster ceilings and miniature proscenium stages.

In the absence of community buildings in the new suburbs, it was the churches which provided a common focus for community activities. The diocese of Exeter, the Roman Catholic Church and the Baptists all built new churches, partly as reparations for war-damaged buildings in the city centre but also to serve totally new parishes. For example, the modest Morice Baptist Church on Ham Drive by Louis de Soissons (1953–4) served the population moved from Morice Town in Devonport which was considered to be one of the worst slums in the city. As the new district became more established, a larger church was built next door designed by Richard Fraser of the de Soissons office, completed in 1962 (Fig 64). This had a pyramidal copper roof and flèche, characteristic of his two earlier churches in the city centre, and he designed the larger Baptist church at Crownhill and the Catholic church of St Teresa at Efford (1958), this also with a spire, but in zinc. St Teresa's was otherwise in unassuming brick, as were the two churches on the greens at Ernesettle and Whitleigh (by Body, Son & Fleury (1953) and Fouracre, Stilwell & Luxton (1955–6) respectively). More sophisticated was St James the Less at Ham by Evans & Sloggett (1957–8) which was a charming stripped classical essay in decorated brick and stone, also with a copper roof and a copper 'Scandinavian' bell tower. The nave was formed from concrete portal frames painted blue and white, focussing on the huge east window designed by Sir Ninian Comper (Fig 65). Comper's iconography was conventionally

Figure 64
Morice Baptist Church, Ham Drive, Ham.
The first church of 1953–4 (right) and the second of 1962 (left).
Louis de Soissons RA & Partners, 1953–4;
Louis de Soissons, Peacock, Hodges, Robertson & Fraser, 1962.

representational, but, as in the city centre, the suburban churches were also supporters of more modern, abstract art. Charles Norris, a monk from Buckfast Abbey, produced abstract coloured glass windows for many Plymouth churches including Walls & Pearn's St Paul, Efford (1962–3) and Evans & Powell's St Peter, Crownhill (1967–70). St Paul's was a plain box of concrete and brick with an interesting concrete diagrid ceiling; St Peter's was circular in plan and was a clear expression of the influence of the Liturgical Movement, bringing

Figure 65
St James the Less, Ham Drive, Ham.
Interior of nave showing east window by
Sir Ninian Comper, 1958.
Evans & Sloggett, 1957–8.

the altar forward to the congregation as had been demonstrated in Frederick
Gibberd's Liverpool Catholic Cathedral (1960–7). The most convincing fusion
of architecture and art was in the exceptional Church of the Ascension at
Crownhill designed in 1956–8 by Potter & Hare of Salisbury (Fig 66 and
see Fig 85). This too brought the altar forward but covered it with a domed
ciborium supported on gilded columns, with a representation of the four
elements by Robert Medley, professor at the Slade School of Art. The abstract
glass in the hexagonal windows behind the altar was by Geoffrey Clarke from
the Royal College of Art and Charles Norris added a crucifix of steel and glass

Figure 66
Church of the Ascension, Crownhill. Nave looking
east showing the ciborium by Robert Medley, 1958.
Potter & Hare, 1956–8.
[DP082246]

in 1976. The blood-red, undulating concrete nave roof was supported on slender precast concrete columns, reminiscent of those at Coventry Cathedral, but, externally, the church was made of reclaimed stone with a great overhanging pitched roof and a separate hexagonal campanile that formed the porch to the nave.

Employment and the completion of the suburbs

A Plan for Plymouth placed new industry around Millbay docks, south of Union Street. But by 1946 the Board of Trade was looking for suitable sites for new industries to replace jobs lost from the Devonport dockyard and, presumably influenced by the Garden City model, these were found adjacent to the new suburbs. The new industries were based on light engineering, clothing and foodstuffs which brought women into the civilian workforce for the first time. By 1948, Bush Radio (to become Rank, the largest television manufacturers in Europe) with a factory by Fuller, Hall & Foulsham, was established at Ernesettle between the houses and the Tamar estuary. Tecalemit Engineering, by Mills, Gallannaugh & Walls at Marsh Mills, anticipated the A38 Parkway and Berketex, the dressmakers, at Honicknowle, reused the government training centre in the old quarry. By the late 1950s, encouraged by government development area grants, a further 17 factories and 10,000 more jobs were created including Clarks Shoes between Whitleigh and Crownhill and Slumberland beds at Ernesettle. The only new factory on Union Street was Jaeger clothing and that was not built until 1960–4.

At Southway, the northernmost and last Abercrombie suburb to be planned and built, industry formed a precinct of its own at the east end adjacent to the Tavistock road. Southway (1955–69) was the only suburb totally conceived under Stirling's regime and was intended to be self-contained with some 2,300 houses, employment and all community facilities (Fig 67). Although it was still centred on the schools and the ribbon access roads were similar to previous suburbs, it was the first suburb to be designed for the private motor car, introducing a version of Radburn planning which had become standard for the new towns – Stevenage, Harlow, Basildon and others – around London. The influential 'ideal suburb' of Radburn, New Jersey, had

Figure 67
Aerial view of Southway showing the stepped terraces of houses with 'catslide' roofs, parking courts and Radburn layout. 'Point blocks' of five-storey flats edge Kinniard Crescent, c 1966.
[NMR/26400/009]

been conceived in the 1920s on a system of vehicle cul-de-sacs serving houses which faced onto continuous greenspace, intended to give safe pedestrian routes without crossing roads. Stirling turned the houses so that they ran up rather than along the contours, facing footpaths and lawns. The houses, flat roofed and cubic in form, stepped up the slopes in long terraces and later versions introduced 'catslide' roofs which presumably simplified the many abutments. Later phases introduced houses with garages and parking courts and small 'point blocks' of flats. Southway also had its own shopping precinct (with a supermarket, shops and banks) around a pedestrian square, a clinic, a branch library, two public houses, two churches and a youth centre.

By 1964, Plymouth had exceeded its housing target with some 13,500 council houses, 3,500 private houses and 850 houses built by the Admiralty. Between 1951 and 1957 over 1,000 council houses were built every year and the completion of Plymouth's 10,000th council dwelling was celebrated in 1954. Ernesettle, consisting of 1,160 houses, was completed by 1953 and Laing's had completed their 1,000th 'Easiform' house by January 1951. The first houses in Whitleigh were occupied in August 1950, in Ernesettle in 1948 and in Ham and Efford in late 1946, only two years after the publication of *A Plan for Plymouth*. Over half of Plymouth's schools were built during the 1950s and 1960s. Together with the roads, sewers, landscape, schools, community buildings, churches and factories, the design and production of the Abercrombie suburbs equal the achievement of the building of the city centre. They demonstrate a pragmatic mixture of Utopian theory from Howard, Mumford and Abercrombie himself, of political aspirations from the post-war Labour government and a peculiarly English assimilation of the picturesque and the practical.

4
Completing the *Plan* and its significance

At Plymouth – the city centre and the suburbs – Abercrombie and Paton Watson created the greatest post-war plan in Britain. It was not a modernist plan in the form then being fashioned by Le Corbusier at Saint-Dié in France (Fig 68) and Chandigarh in India nor was it based on the megalomaniac monumental plans of the pre-war European dictators. Rather, it signalled the last in a long tradition of humanistic city planning that had begun in the Renaissance and had been formalised in the 19th century. It was the last great Beaux-Arts city plan yet it represented, more than any other, the city of the Welfare State. It was new, clean, regular and, above all, optimistic. It was intended to be democratic and non-hierarchical – its streets were open to everybody, its open spaces and parks healthy, its buildings communal and its plan ordered. It was designed for an equally ordered society which had been given the opportunity to devote itself to education, work and culture. It presupposed a national and local government that was altruistic and a society that would appreciate the new world that was being created in its name.

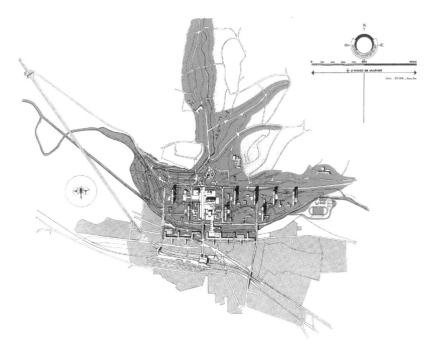

Great Square, Armada Way. Pearl Assurance (left) and Dingles department store (right) in the background.
[DP086692]

Figure 68 (right)
Le Corbusier's Plan of the reconstruction of Saint-Dié, 1945. Eight 'Unité' blocks of flats are placed orthogonally with a central civic precinct within an open landscape. The area south of the River Meurthe (shaded grey) was not destroyed.
[© FLC/ ADAGP, Paris and DACS, London 2010]

Of course, Plymouth was one of many British cities that were being rebuilt and across the Channel most of Europe was rebuilding itself. Of British cities, only Plymouth renewed the whole of its city centre and its institutions. Most cities were only partly damaged so that in Coventry, the city that most resembled Plymouth, for example, Georgian buildings near the cathedral, the banks and the old town hall were retained and the new plan formed around them. Coventry, Exeter, Hull, Southampton and Bristol (in the form of its new shopping precinct at Broadmead) all reconfigured their existing street layouts and added very little that was actually new. Donald Gibson, the city architect for Coventry, designed a major new axis similar in principle to Armada Way, and before *A Plan for Plymouth* (Fig 69). The axis was focussed on the ruined cathedral spire, but it and its cross axes had no other foci so that the new rectilinear geometry was unresolved against the existing curved streets. Thomas Sharp's plan for Exeter of 1946 which set up only one new street – Princesshay – also focussed on the cathedral. Sharp's notion was that only

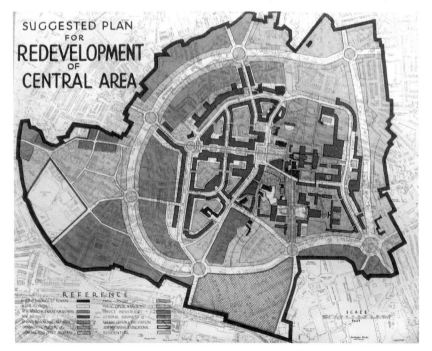

Figure 69 (left)
Donald Gibson's Suggested plan for redevelopment of central area. *The axis through the Upper and Lower shopping precincts and major new road cross at the cathedral spire (added by the author).*
[Coventry City Council 1945 The Future Coventry. *Reproduced by permission of the Conservation and Archaeology Team, Coventry City Council]*

Figure 70 (right, above)
Thomas Sharp's Redevelopment in the cathedral area, Exeter, 1946. *This shows the 'shopping precinct' (Princesshay) as a pedestrianised street focussed on the cathedral, and the existing High Street widened with new arcaded shops (shown in red).*
[Sharp, T 1946 Exeter Phoenix: A Plan for Rebuilding. *London: Architectural Press, 103]*

Figure 71 (right, below)
The town as a whole, 1947. This shows the centre of an old town revised into functional precincts with shops and business in the centre and housing on the periphery, all served with new ring roads.
[Ministry of Town and Country Planning 1947 The Redevelopment of Central Areas. *London: HMSO, 19]*

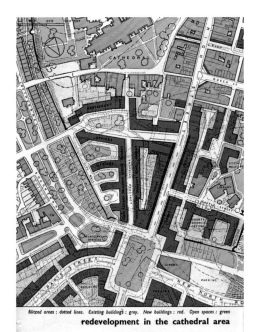

Blitzed areas : dotted lines. Existing buildings : grey. New buildings : red. Open spaces : green
redevelopment in the cathedral area

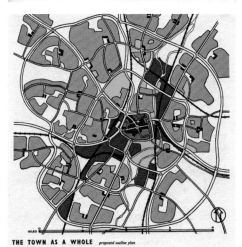

THE TOWN AS A WHOLE *proposed outline plan*

- shops
- business
- industry and railway land
- educational, recreational and public buildings
- residential
- open space

glimpses of the cathedral would be revealed, following the picturesque view of historic cities of his *English Panorama* of 1936. His only grand gesture was to widen the existing High Street to form a new shopping precinct (Fig 70). On the continent, the pioneer modernist architect, Auguste Perret, planned Le Havre (1945–54) with a regular grid of streets and consistent concrete-framed blocks, closely resembling Plymouth.

All the city plans had similarities. They all imposed single-function precincts, removed housing from their centres, reduced densities, invented new parks, created new suburbs and built new ring roads. This was no coincidence for the theory and practice of replanning cities was centrally directed by the Ministry of Town & Country Planning which published its policy, *The Redevelopment of Central Areas*, in 1947. This was heavily influenced by the plans of Plymouth and Coventry and behind them and the ministry hovers the figure of Abercrombie. His pupil from Liverpool, William Holford, advised the ministry, Donald Gibson had taught at the Liverpool School in the 1930s and one of his assistants at Coventry until 1940, Percy Johnson-Marshall, who later joined the MTCP, was another Liverpool graduate. Plymouth may be seen not only as the single city plan by Abercrombie to be realised but also as the important precedent for a system of planning which literally changed the face of post-war Britain (Fig 71). The greatest obvious change was in planning for the motor car. The motor car was regarded as a necessary danger to be separated from pedestrians – hence Radburn planning and Alker Tripp's precincts. The inner ring roads may have had their origins in Parisian boulevards or the Ringstrasse in Vienna, but the exponential increase in vehicle ownership through the 1950s and 1960s and the consequent rise in the political importance of the motor industry and the highways engineer, changed the perceived scale of the problem. Gibson's ring road in Coventry was drawn as a boulevard but under subsequent planners and under the influence of Colin Buchanan's *Traffic in Towns* of 1963, it became an urban motorway with underpasses, overpasses and clover-leaf junctions. The same was true for Bristol where the inner ring road, planned in the 1930s as the result of Abercrombie's *Regional Plan*, sliced through the Georgian Queen Square and cruelly separated the eastern suburbs from the centre with a vast dual carriageway. The Plymouth ring road remained at-grade and became neither a motorway nor the intended tree-lined boulevard but, with its many railing barriers and gloomy pedestrian underpasses, it too divorced the city centre from its suburbs.

Sharp's Princesshay, realised from 1949–56, and Frederick Gibberd's Lansbury shopping centre (1949–51), designed for the 'Live Architecture' exhibition for the Festival, were the first pedestrianised shopping streets in Britain. More radical was Gibson's shopping precinct in Coventry which was totally pedestrianised – two rectangular precincts on the axis were surrounded by arcaded shops on two levels, inspired by the Rows at Chester. Although the Coventry precincts were not finished until 1959, the drawings and models were published and the idea was much copied, especially for the new towns of Stevenage, Harlow and Crawley. By the early 1950s, there were other important built examples from Europe. The Lijnbaan in Rotterdam (1951–3) by Van den Broek & Bakema consisted of a long, narrow pedestrian shopping street traversed by trafficked streets, rather like a thin version of Armada Way (Fig 72). The centre of the new satellite town of Vällingby (1952–4) near Stockholm by the city planning director, Sven Markelius, was totally pedestrianised and seemed to have all the community facilities of a perfect Abercrombie neighbourhood unit (Fig 73). The shopping streets of Vällingby and the Lijnbaan were single use, but in both places mass housing (flats in point blocks), offices, cinemas and churches, all planned together, were within easy walking distance. This was an important difference, for the low-density suburbs of the British cities were a very long way from their city centres. At the end of the working day, the civic and shopping precincts were deserted, prompting the *Daily Mail* to report that Plymouth city centre was '… a world built, at its heart at least, for office workers and shopkeepers. People came from as far away as Penzance to shop. But no-one lives above the shops, no children play, no music wafts down from sitting rooms. The centre of Plymouth at night is as dead as the empty square mile which is the City of London.'[12]

Similar criticism prompted Arthur Ling, Gibson's successor at Coventry, to introduce two tower blocks of housing and an office tower into the shopping precinct in 1962. Exeter, Broadmead and Plymouth (with the exception of Frankfort Gate) stuck inflexibly to their original zones. The new architecture was also similar in the new cities. It was all rigidly predetermined by the local authorities and made of consistent materials with Nash's Regent Street and Georgian London or Bath frequently quoted as precedents. Exeter and Coventry

Figure 72
The Lijnbaan shopping street,
Rotterdam, The Netherlands.
Van den Broek & Bakema, 1951–3.

Figure 73
Vällingby town centre, Sweden.
Paving in three colours of granite by
Erik Glemme.
Sven Markelius, planner, 1952–4.

Figure 74
The Pavilions (incorporating a concert hall,
swimming pool and ice rink) with the Duke of
Cornwall Hotel, Millbay Road in the background.
Module 2 Designers, 1991.

were in brick and Broadmead, initially, in Bath stone. Like Plymouth, the buildings were derived from classical models and were cubic in form, flat roofed with square openings, often framed with contrasting stone or slate. They too were intended to be neutral backdrops to the shops and human activities.

Completing the Plymouth plan 1962–2006

With the completion of the Civic Centre, the opening of the Tamar road bridge, the suburbs finished and Southway well under way, 1962 marks the end of the reconstruction of Plymouth. The Reconstruction Committee was disbanded in 1961 and the completion of the *Plan* was left to the short-term demands of developers and party politics. The city centre survives in a form that Abercrombie and Paton Watson would still recognise. This is perhaps surprising for many decisions were taken to dilute it. The concert hall, the unsightly Pavilions (Fig 74), was built outside the entertainments precinct and the *Western Morning News* moved to the northern suburbs. The Odeon Cinema in New George Street closed in 1960, while the Drake Cinema on Derry's Cross was demolished in 2002 (Fig 75) to be replaced by the new multiplex cinema at

Figure 75
Drake Cinema (later Drake Odeon), Derry's Cross/
Union Street (demolished 2002).
Leonard Allen, 1956–8.

Coxside, accessible only by car. A casino replaced the Drake Cinema and a budget hotel partly filled Derry's Cross, crudely blocking the axis from the Athenaeum to Raleigh Street. Sir Percy Thomas's neat Methodist church (Fig 76) and the exceptional 1950s Turnbull's Garage on Charles Cross have been demolished. A hotel was built at the north end of Armada Way and another, the Holiday Inn (1970), was built at the Hoe. Both are made of clumsy concrete blocks and panels and the Holiday Inn obstructs the vista of the Hoe and makes an uneasy rival to the elegant profile of the Civic Centre (Fig 77). The Drake Circus shopping centre has been rebuilt twice. The first, opened in 1971, looked inwards to an open precinct. The second, designed in the 1980s but not built until 2002–6, was based on the American mall. It internalised the process of shopping and deliberately turned its back on the rest of the city

Figure 76
King Street (later Wesley) Methodist Church,
The Crescent (demolished c 2002).
Sir Percy Thomas & Son, 1956–7.

(Fig 78). Its many materials lack the uniformity of Paton Watson's Plymouth and its privatised mall is the converse of Abercrombie's egalitarian streets. The only important new building has been the Theatre Royal (1978–82), appropriately in the entertainments precinct at Derry's Cross, designed by Peter Moro who had been responsible for the Festival Hall in 1951 (Fig 79). It is especially impressive at night with the foyers visible through the great glass walls along Royal Parade.

The parking problem was 'solved' by building multi-storey car parks – between Cornwall Street and Mayflower Street, beyond Frankfort Gate and behind the Civic Centre. With the regularisation of car parking came the call for pedestrianisation of the city centre. From the 1980s, the original traffic

Figure 77
The tower of the Holiday Inn Hotel dominates this part of the Hoe – Civic Centre tower, Guildhall tower and Church of Christ the King are in the background.
Alan J Wyatt, 1970.

Figure 78
Drake Circus shopping centre, Old Town Street/
Exeter Street/Charles Street.
Chapman Taylor LLP, 2002–6.

pattern and kerbs were replaced by a plethora of different landscape materials and features of every conceivable type. The paving, distantly copied from Vällingby, was often curved in a misguided attempt to be informal and deliberately ignored the patterns, rhythms and materials of the original architecture. The new landscape was suburban in concept and scale and blocked the Beaux-Arts vistas in Armada Way and the cross streets.

The original architecture soon became out of fashion. As incremental changes occurred – shopfronts altered, upper windows blocked, signs added, flagpoles removed or awnings discontinued – the architecture was coarsened

Figure 79
Theatre Royal, Royal Parade.
Peter Moro Partnership, 1978–82.

and tenants and the public valued it less. Almost all of the shop interiors were changed and changed again. Foyers of banks, for example, Lloyds and the National Provincial, were floored in and fine interiors such as that at the Post Office on St Andrew's Cross disappeared for ever. After 50 years, the thin, elegant metal windows began to fail and were replaced in clumsy white plastic to different patterns. Inexcusably, the exterior of the Pannier Market was altered and modish porches and features added.

On the positive side, Plymouth rediscovered its waterfront. Abercrombie had assumed that the commercial and naval uses of the waterfront would

continue unchanged and that only the Hoe would be used for leisure. The
Barbican, which Abercrombie had wished to conserve, was threatened with
demolition in the mid-1950s, ostensibly on the grounds of slum clearance. For
the first time, there was organised local opposition – from the Junior Chamber
of Commerce, the hastily formed Plymouth Barbican Association and the
Society for the Protection of Ancient Buildings. Gordon Cullen reported that
the area was 'a living, developing organism of ordinary hard-working folk'.[13]
The result was that old buildings were gradually repaired and, as the fishing
industry declined, the area became a magnet for tourism with the cafés, bars
and restaurants that the city centre lacked (Fig 80). The scene was radically
improved in the 1990s when the Sutton Harbour Company installed a lock gate
and created a 'floating' harbour, used as a marina and for fishing boats. Around
the harbour the company developed a residential district for a new clientele
with the first large-scale private housing in the city centre (Fig 81). Public
pressure reopened the Tinside Pool below the Hoe and public access was
gained to the Royal William Yard, relinquished by the Navy and developed into
private flats and offices. The harbour at Millbay, however, remained stubbornly
derelict despite the ferries across to France and Spain.

Figure 80
Barbican and Sutton Harbour – cafés, restaurants
and bars around the main tourist area of the city.
[© Silverport Pictures, 0808020266]

Figure 81
Pinnacle Quay flats, Sutton Harbour.
Form Design Group Architects, 2004.

Figure 82
Blandford Road, Efford. BISF Type A houses on right,
c 1949.

The suburbs survived remarkably. Lasdun's footbridge at Whitleigh was replaced but otherwise only the Cornish Units failed seriously and their lower floors were 're-skinned' in brick. As in the city centre, the thin metal windows were substituted for plastic in different patterns. The greatest change to the housing was brought about by the 'right to buy' in the 1980s. Adding porches and extensions altered the consistency or monotony of the original to give a spurious individuality that it had never had. Car ownership in the 1960s made up for inadequate public transport, but none of the houses had garages (except at Southway) and parked cars filled every street (Fig 82). Greater mobility meant that shopping in the city centre or elsewhere was possible and the neighbourhood centres faded. The suburbs were too dispersed and at too low a density to support them, although this was exacerbated by the city's inability to build all the facilities that had been planned. The churches and the public houses declined, partly for the same reasons. Falling congregations resulted in the demolition of St Teresa and St Paul at Efford and churches on Ham Green and Whitleigh Green were replaced. In the 1980s and 1990s, the pattern of shopping changed again with the establishment of out-of-town supermarkets at Marsh Mills, in the quarry at Honicknowle, at Estover and Roborough (Fig 83). The new supermarkets and retail 'parks' of the A38 concealed another change – that of declining employment. The manufacturing of the 1950s struggled to compete in the new global workplace and Tecalamit, Clarks, Berketex and Jaeger and many of the light engineering firms all closed. Jobs were partly replaced by the expanding university, conveniently placed on the old technical college site north of the city centre, and by 'high-tech' industries on the Science Park south of the airport or in far Belliver. But the greatest asset of the Plymouth suburbs remained their landscape and gardens. Abercrombie's recommendation to build on the high ground and to reserve the valleys as woodland, gave the suburbs a distinct and individual bosky character very different from contemporary estates in Coventry, Southampton or south Bristol (Fig 84).

The other post-war cities fared worse. Sharp's Princesshay was demolished in 2002 to make way for a more sophisticated and far denser shopping centre. Broadmead, never a great architectural success, added the Galleries shopping centre (1986–91), another version of the American mall, but this time on three levels. Later, it knocked down all the eastern part of the original layout and vastly expanded into Cabot Circus (2003–8), giving Bristol the dubious

Figure 83
Sainsbury's supermarket, Marsh Mills.
Dixon Jones Architects, 1991–4.
[AA023631]

Figure 84
Aerial view of Southway looking east. Southway Comprehensive School (now Southway Community College) being rebuilt in 2009 in the foreground and factories in the distance; the nine 'point blocks' along Kinnaird Crescent look north to the countryside and dense woods separate Southway from Crownhill to the south.
[NMR/26400/011]

distinction of being the only city in Britain to expand its inner ring road. Coventry, under successive planners, went on developing its plan but its clarity quickly eroded. The open space of Broadgate was filled in with the dim Cathedral Lanes shopping centre (1986) that blocked the axis to the cathedral. The West Orchards shopping centre (1986), yet another internalised mall, was added to the main cross street and, like Drake Circus, stole land from the original public street. Much worse, new access escalators filled the middle of the Upper Precinct and the original access stairs were demolished. The Lower Precinct was clumsily roofed over in glass, its access ramps removed and the original arcades filled in. Of the post-war cities, only Plymouth attracted work by nationally significant architects. Many of the commercial buildings of Exeter, Coventry and, especially, Broadmead were consistently worthy but rather dull. The exception was the competition for Coventry Cathedral. Basil Spence's wonderful new building (1951–62) captured the public imagination and, because of this, it was Coventry, rather than Plymouth, that became the national symbol of revival and reconciliation. Plymouth was eclipsed and its significance forgotten.

5

The conservation of the *Plan*

Plymouth is the most complete and sole surviving British post-war plan. It is as important and representative of its time as Georgian Bath or medieval York are of theirs and therefore its future and conservation are as vital as it is in those ancient cities. Plymouth, now more than 50 years old, can be regarded as an historic city. But Plymouth is a work-a-day city and its accretions and shabbiness obscure its real face. There is a lack of understanding and pride in the extraordinary achievement of the 1950s, not helped by architectural historians who too easily ignore it or look back sentimentally to a golden past. For example, the historian Gavin Stamp writing of Britain's 'lost' cities:

> What, after so much wartime suffering, was achieved was a new city centre which was so inadequate, so lacking in proper urban density and so mediocre in its architecture that the 1950s buildings are now being replaced. …modern Plymouth is a tragedy, and it is impossible not to grieve for the messy, imperfect but fascinating and elegant city that stood between the Hamoaze and the Cattewater before the Second World War.[14]

There is a feeling in Plymouth, prevalent from the 1960s, that somehow the new city was not quite good enough and that the only way to correct this would be to knock it down and start again. Perhaps this attitude is something of a tradition in Plymouth informed as it is by the certainties of military command. The stained stonework and the rusting metal windows can be repaired, but the architecture and the place need to be valued before such efforts can be justified. There is no amenity society fighting for its preservation, and, until very recently, no guidebook to the 1950s city.[15] For the tourist, Plymouth still remains the city of Drake and the *Mayflower*.

Attitudes to 1950s buildings are changing as they changed towards Victorian and Modernist buildings in the later 20th century. One of the difficulties is that the late classicism of the 1950s has never been recognised as a distinctive style. It was disliked by the architectural press and therefore seldom published and contemporary architectural historians were intent on linking the heroic period of early Modernism to the New Brutalism of the 1950s, missing out any 'aberrations' which had arrived at the same time. However, many 1950s buildings are listed by the Secretary of State for Culture, Media and Sport as buildings of special architectural or historic interest, demonstrating 'that the best of modern architecture ranks with that of the past, and will equally stand

Aerial view of city centre looking south. Armada Way from North Cross roundabout and the University, bottom left, to the Hoe with the Naval Memorial, Smeaton's Tower and Tinside Lido, top right. The civic precinct with the Civic Centre and Guildhall, centre, Derry's Cross and the Pannier Market, centre right, and the new Drake Circus shopping precinct, centre left. The Barbican and Sutton Harbour under the walled Citadel, top left. [NMR/26408/031]

the test of time'.[16] In Plymouth, the Civic Centre, the Guildhall, Barclays and the National Provincial banks, the Pannier Market, the Unitarian, Baptist and Catholic churches and the Church of the Ascension (Fig 85) are all listed and the Great Square is on the *Register of Parks and Gardens*.[17] Plymouth has more listed 1950s buildings than any other provincial city. In addition, Plymouth had more 1950s buildings designed by contemporary recipients of the Royal Gold Medal for Architecture than any other city – Giles Gilbert Scott (1925), Percy Thomas (1939), W Curtis Green (1942), Howard Robertson (1949), J Murray Easton (1955) and Abercrombie (1946). If one adds the architects Thomas Tait, Louis de Soissons, Geoffrey Jellicoe and William Crabtree and artists Bainbridge Copnall, Robert Medley, Hans Feibusch, William McMillan, Hans Tisdall, John Piper and Patrick Reyntiens, one has a list of some of the best known and most significant cultural figures of the mid-century. Add to that list the little known 'local heroes' like Walls & Pearn, Alec French, David Weeks, Charles Norris, Edward Narracott and the city architect and unique masterpieces like Sherren's National Provincial Bank and Messrs Joseph's NAAFI, and one realises what a rich and diverse building culture the 1950s brought to Plymouth. No doubt there are more buildings worthy of listing.

However, single buildings do not make a place. The grid plan of Plymouth has always been regarded with suspicion. The idea of a Grand Plan is alien to the national psyche, steeped as it is in notions of the picturesque and the informal. Yet, despite the fact that it remained unfinished and notwithstanding the many changes over the years, the *Plan* has proved itself to be robust and has always functioned well. The fashions for pedestrian precincts and covered malls, often driven by self-interested retailers, have come and gone but the street persists. The architect and urbanist David Mackay, who planned the Olympic village and port for Barcelona in 1992, wrote:

> The street is the backbone of our society. For a society is not solely about individual freedom, it is about the freedom to associate with others and to enjoy the unexpected encounter. …The street gives a recognisable form to public space where people can seek out their markets and, in the course of their search, acquire unexpected information – be it in a new product in a shop window or a chance meeting with a friend.[18]

Figure 85
Church of the Ascension, Crownhill. The church from the south-west showing the separate campanile. Listed Grade II in 1998. Potter & Hare, 1956–8. [DP082231]

Mackay was appointed to prepare a new urban plan for Plymouth, the first outside consultant since Abercrombie, and his *A Vision for Plymouth* was presented in 2004 (Fig 86). Mackay examined the problems of the city centre, but stressed the importance of the grid plan:

> Watson and Abercrombie's plan for the City Centre was a masterpiece of modern English town planning. It must be conserved, not as a fossil but in an invigorated form that responds to present circumstances and shifts in cultural values…. Our response to this opportunity should not be constrained by protectionist policies: the nature of the grid structure must be respected, but the plots can be rebuilt to a greater density, and the new cross-streets can provide the permeability that Watson and Abercrombie originally wanted for the city centre.[19]

Figure 86
City centre plan from A Vision for Plymouth.
[Mackay, Zogolovitch and Harradine 2004, 62–3. Reproduced by permission of MBM Arquitectes, AZ Urban Studio and Plymouth 2020]

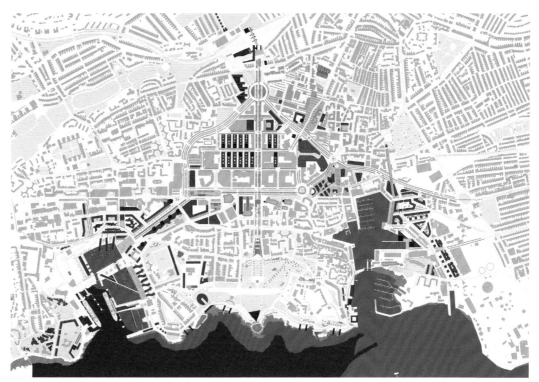

Mackay identified the dominance of the ring road and its excessive traffic speeds, the highway design and the cluttered landscape of Armada Way and the cross streets as problems which could be solved easily. He redrew the ring road as a tree-lined boulevard with at-grade pedestrian crossings relating to all the cross streets, connecting the city centre to its suburbs. The road swung north of the Charles Church, thereby reuniting the church with the Barbican. He proposed a new, open landscape for Armada Way that cleared all the accretions and re-established the central axis and view (Fig 87). Armada Way was extended to the railway station and Abercrombie's waterfall above Notte Street was redrawn, to entice pedestrians from the Great Square onto the Hoe. Mackay also addressed the issues of the low density of the northern part of the centre and the single-use zones. Between New George Street, Cornwall Street and Mayflower Street he drew a new plan of building blocks which respected Abercrombie's building lines but introduced a series of north–south streets which greatly improved the permeability of this part of the city and the opportunities for shopfronts. For Cornwall Street, he proposed a series of taller, denser blocks of shopping, housing and other uses, abandoning the strict zoning of the original city (Fig 88). Mackay stressed the need for the city to exploit its 'enviable location' along the waterfront. Therefore he proposed new connections along the waters' edge and back into the city with the Hoe as a pivotal revitalised attraction. *A Vision for Plymouth* was specifically not a conservation plan, but it recognised the essence of the Abercrombie idea. In 2004, the city removed the underpass under Royal Parade, introduced a level crossing and repaved Armada Way from the Great Square to New George Street. A grand new space was rediscovered, a vindication of Mackay's *Vision* and of Abercrombie's *Plan* (Fig 89).

However, since 2004 Mackay's proposals have not progressed. The simple idea which underpins the Mackay plan of both conservation *and* development based on Abercrombie's *Plan* has not been grasped, despite its great potential

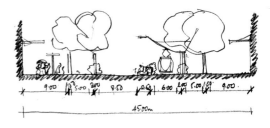

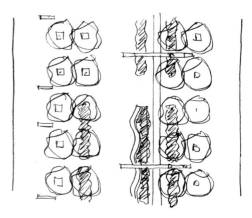

Figure 87
The proposed changes to 'improve the system of movement and civic scale' on Armada Way from A Vision for Plymouth. *The central space is kept clear with a light rail transport system between avenues of trees. The pavements adjacent to the shops are widened.*
[Mackay, Zogolovitch and Harradine 2004, 74. Reproduced by permission of MBM Arquitectes, AZ Urban Studio and Plymouth 2020]

Figure 88
Proposed new living quarter for Cornwall Street from A Vision for Plymouth.
[Mackay, Zogolovitch and Harradine 2004, 65. Reproduced by permission of MBM Arquitectes, AZ Urban Studio and Plymouth 2020]

Figure 89
The repaving of Armada Way and the
Great Square.
Plymouth City Council, 2004.

for regeneration. The significance of the *Plan* and architecture of the city centre needs to be formally recognised to prevent unsuitable opportunistic development and further loss of significant buildings. The necessity for this is acutely demonstrated by the recent demolition of the NAAFI Services' Club. Designation of central Plymouth as a Conservation Area would seem to be the most appropriate way to protect its special interest but, at the very least, proper management of the future centre is essential. Other cities seem more sensitive towards their heritage. Auguste Perret's Le Havre, for example, was declared a World Heritage Site in 2005 and it is a flourishing commercial centre and a tourist attraction. Vällingby has changed and added to its shops, but has done so within the principles of the original plan and has restored its paving, light fittings and other original features. The mixed-use city that the continent regards as normal has formed the basis of many recent successful British developments, for example at Brindley Place in Birmingham or the Quayside in Newcastle upon Tyne. A balance between commerce and conservation is not impossible.

The conservation of the suburbs has not been an issue, simply because their unique qualities have not yet been recognised. The suburbs too would benefit from characterisation studies analysing the spaces, landscape and

Figure 90
Aerial view of Whitleigh Green. New flats and church under construction in 2009 facing the Green (centre). The replacement footbridge from Honicknowle (bottom left) leads to Whitleigh Way. Woodfield Primary School (top right). [NMR/26400/040]

Figure 91 (top)
The corridor space leading to the main hall in Whitleigh
Primary School, Lancaster Gardens, Whitleigh
(demolished 2009).
Louis de Soissons, Peacock, Hodges, Robertson & Fraser,
1956.

Figure 92 (above)
The Tiger public house, Bodmin Road, Whitleigh
(derelict in 2009).
Louis de Soissons, Peacock, Hodges, Robertson & Fraser,
c 1958.

architecture if inappropriate new developments such as the new flats at Ernesettle Green, Whitleigh Green or in Efford are to be avoided (Fig 90). Another significant change has been the rebuilding of the schools, as promised by the Blair government from 1997 and driven by Plymouth becoming a unitary authority. Some 12 per cent of Plymouth's schools have been replaced in the last decade. No doubt the new schools are more efficient in terms of staffing, resources and energy but one wonders what social impact the removal of the heart of these communities might have and it seems a great loss that the delicate architecture of Louis de Soissons in particular has not been more valued (Figs 91 and 92). The suburbs are under other new pressures. Plymouth has been designated by the Department of Communities and Local Government as a Growth Point and the current population of about 250,000 is due to rise to 300,000 by 2026 requiring 30,000 new homes and 42,500 new jobs.[20] The statistics seem strangely familiar. Although some of this population will be outside the current city boundaries and the city has 'brownfield' land at Millbay, Plymstock and Devonport, the suburbs and city centre will have to absorb much of this growth. How this will be achieved without despoiling their character has yet to be defined, but this growth should be seen as an opportunity to introduce a cultural mix that, perhaps, the Abercrombie *Plan* and its zoned precincts always lacked. As David Mackay points out:

> The city must have the confidence to sustain the vision, no matter what pressures are placed upon it as a result of any feeding frenzy among its developer friends. An intensified city means that the parties have a renewed and different sense of responsibility towards each other and to their city. Each developer has a chance of making a heroic contribution to the city. Each development matters, each must build up to the connected, high-quality transformation that the vision articulates.[21]

1950s Plymouth is nationally exceptional and significant and, in developing its future, we should learn from it rather than fight against it. Abercrombie and Paton Watson gave Plymouth a unique form which, once understood and valued, can underpin the city's regeneration. The original plans embody the enlightened and progressive policies of post-war Britain; what it needs now are imaginative, knowledgeable, skilled and sympathetic hands capable of nurturing these important qualities.

Notes

1 Alker Tripp, H 1942 *Town Planning and Road Traffic*. London: Edward Arnold, 17

2 Abercrombie and Paton Watson 1943, 67

3 Abercrombie and Paton Watson 1943, 72
Other areas are 1.6 per cent entertainments, 1.7 per cent car parks, 5.8 per cent station and bus station and 0.9 per cent existing churches.

4 Abercrombie, autobiographical notes, quoted in Gerald Dix 'Patrick Abercrombie 1879–1957' in Cherry, Gordon E 1981 *Pioneers in British Planning*. London: Architectural Press, 114–5

5 Abercrombie and Paton Watson 1943, 77

6 Abercrombie and Paton Watson 1943, 103–4

7 Lewis Mumford *The Culture of Cities* quoted by Abercrombie and Watson 1943, 4

8 Abercrombie and Paton Watson 1943, 81

9 Anonymous tenant in *Echoes of Ernesettle* 2 1992 Exeter: Devon Library Services quoted by Phillips, Hilary 2007 'Suburbia Reconstructed: A Study of Ernesettle' Unpublished MA dissertation, University College Falmouth, 30

10 Mrs Hurst in *Echoes of Ernesettle* 2 1992 Exeter: Devon Library Services quoted by Phillips, Hilary 2007 'Suburbia Reconstructed: A Study of Ernesettle' Unpublished MA dissertation, University College Falmouth, 47

11 Pearn, Ernest J 1989 *Whitleigh: The Troublesome Formative Years* Private printing (Plymouth Local Studies Library), 80

12 Stanley Bennett in the *Daily Mail*, 27 September 1961

13 Cullen, Gordon 1961 'Plymouth Barbican' in *Townscape*. London: Architectural Press reprinted from *Architectural Review* April 1957, 288

14 Stamp, Gavin 2007 *Britain's Lost Cities* London: Aurum, 169

15 See www.20thcenturycity.org.uk an on-line guide developed by the Architecture Centre for Devon and Cornwall with Heritage Lottery Funding in 2009 (accessed 16 August 2010).

16 Alan Howarth, Department for Culture, Media and Sport quoted in Harwood 2003.

17 The Great Square is registered on the *English Heritage Register of Parks and Gardens of Special Historic Interest in England* as the 'Civic Square'. The *Register* consists of over 1,600 designed landscapes of special historic interest representing important design and designers over the centuries. Although inclusion of an historic park or garden on the *Register* in itself brings no additional statutory controls, there is a presumption in favour of their conservation in local planning policy. The Great Square was registered Grade II in 1999 and is one of the few 20th-century gardens registered.

18 Mackay, David 2004 'Recovering a Lost Tradition' in *Footprints in the City*. Catalogue of exhibition at Aedes East, Berlin 7 May–27 June 2004. Berlin: AedesBerlin

19 Mackay, Zogolovitch and Harradine 2004, 48

20 Statistics from Department for Communities and Local Government 2006 *New Growth Points: Partnership Growth with Government: Plymouth*. These figures are slightly amended in Plymouth City Council 2007 *Plymouth New Growth Point: Programme of Development 2006 to 2026*

21 Mackay, Zogolovitch, and Harradine 2004, 98

References and further reading

Abercrombie, Patrick and Paton Watson, James 1943 *A Plan for Plymouth*. Plymouth: Underhill

Architecture Centre for Devon and Cornwall, Plymouth: 20th century city, www.20thcenturycity.org.uk

Chalkey, Brian, Dunkerley, David and Gripaios, Peter 1991 *Plymouth: Maritime City in Transition*. Newton Abbot: David & Charles

Cherry, Bridget and Pevsner, Nikolaus 1989 *The Buildings of England – Devon*. Harmondsworth: Penguin. Plymouth, 631–82

Craigie, Jill 1946 *The Way we Live*. Film for Two Cities Films

Harwood, Elain 2003 *England: A Guide to Post-War Listed Buildings*. London: Batsford

Mackay, David (MBM Arquitectes), Zogolovitch, Roger and Harradine, Martin (AZ Urban Studio) 2004 *A Vision for Plymouth*. Plymouth: University of Plymouth

Plymouth Barbican Association, South West Image Bank, http://swib.wikidot.com (accessed 16 August 2010)

Plymouth and West Devon Record Office, www.plymouth.gov.uk/archives (accessed 16 August 2010)

Richardson, A E and Lovett, Gill C 1924 *Regional Architecture of the West of England*. London: Ernest Benn Ltd. Plymouth, Stonehouse and Devonport, 45–77

Robinson, Chris 2008 *Plymouth in the Twenties and Thirties*. Plymouth: Pen & Ink Publishing

Twyford, H P (revised by Robinson, Chris) 2005 *It Came to Our Door*. Plymouth: Pen & Ink Publishing (first published 1945)

Wasley, Gerald 2008 *Plymouth A Shattered City: The story of Hilter's attack on Plymouth and its people 1939–45*. Wellington: Halsgrove (first published 1991)

Other titles in the Informed Conservation series

The Informed Conservation series highlights the special character of some of our most important historic areas and the development pressures they are facing. There are over 20 titles in the series, some looking at whole towns such as Berwick upon Tweed, while others focus on particular building types such as historic warehouses in Manchester and Liverpool. The books are written in an engaging style and include high-quality colour photographs and specially commissioned graphics. Further information on other titles in the Informed Conservation series can be found in the publications section on our website www.english-heritage.org.uk.

Plymouth city centre

KEY

1. Braille Garden, Armada Way
   H J W Stirling, city architect and
   J Paton Watson, city engineer
   (c 1958)

2. Frankfort Gate
   H J W Stirling, city architect
   in association with Sydney
   Greenwood, John Laing Easiform
   (1955–7)

3. Pannier Market, Cornwall Street/
   Frankfort Gate/New George Street
   Walls & Pearn (1956–9)
   Listed Grade II

4. Regent/Odeon Cinema, New
   George Street
   H J Hammick (1931, demolished
   1963)

5. Nos 72–8 New George Street
   William Crabtree and executive
   architects (1949–52)

6. Marks & Spencer, Cornwall Street/
   Old Town Street (now within Drake
   Circus shopping centre)
   Lewis & Hickey (1949–51)

7. Burton's, Old Town Street/
   Eastlake Street
   N Martin, staff architect to
   Montague Burton (1949–52,
   demolished 2002)

8. Boots, New George Street/
   Old Town Street
   C St C Oakes, staff architect to
   Boots Pure Drug Co (1950–3)

9. Drake Circus shopping centre
   (shown dotted)
   Chapman Taylor LLP (1989 and
   2002–6)

10. Charles Church, Charles Cross
    (1640–58, tower 1708, spire 1766,
    damaged 1941)

11. Westminster House (bank), Old
    Town Street
    Body, Son & Fleury (1955–c 1958)

12. Plymouth Co-operative Society
    store, New George Street/
    Raleigh Street/Royal Parade
    W J Reed, staff architect to
    Co-operative Wholesale Society
    (1950–2)

    Co-operative Insurance Society,
    New George Street
    W J Reed succeeded by R C
    Steel (1960–1)

13. *Western Morning News* office,
    New George Street
    Herbert O Ellis & Clarke (1937–9)

14. Pearl Assurance House offices,
    Royal Parade/Armada Way
    Alec F French in association with
    Sir John Burnet Tait & Partners
    (1950–2)

15. Dingles department store, Royal
    Parade/Armada Way
    Thomas S Tait of Sir John Burnet
    Tait & Partners (1949–51)

16. Dolcis, New George Street
    Ellis E Somake, staff architect to
    Upson's Ltd (1949–51)

17. No 11 and Nos 15–17 New
    George Street
    Edgar Catchpole, city architect
    and Arthur J Ardin (1955–6)

    No 19 New George Street
    Edgar Catchpole, city architect
    and Edward Narracott (1954–5)

18. Lloyds Bank and Popham's
    department store, Royal Parade
    Easton & Robertson (1955–7)

19. Norwich Union House offices,
    Old Town Street/Royal Parade
    Donald Hamilton Wakeford &
    Partners (1950–2)

20. South Western Gas Board offices,
    Derry's Cross
    Whinney, Son & Austen Hall
    (1954–c 1958)

21. Drake Cinema (later Drake
    Odeon), Derry's Cross
    Leonard Allen (1956–8,
    demolished c 2000)

22. Theatre Royal, Derry's Cross/
    Royal Parade
    Peter Moro Partnership (1978–82)

23. Civic Centre, Armada Way/
    Royal Parade
    H J W Stirling, city architect
    (1954–7) succeeded by Allan
    Ballantyne of Jellicoe Ballantyne &
    Coleridge (1957–62)
    Listed Grade II

24. Crown Courts and police station,
    Armada Way/Princess Street
    H J W Stirling, city architect,
    executed by Jellicoe Ballantyne &
    Coleridge (1960–3)

25. Guildhall, Royal Parade/
    Armada Way
    Norman & Hine with E Godwin
    (1870–4) rebuilt by H J W Stirling,
    city architect (1954–9)
    Listed Grade II

26. St Andrew's Church, Royal Parade
    Rebuilt by Frederick Etchells
    (1948–57)
    Listed Grade I

27. Royal Insurance offices,
    St Andrew's Cross
    Alec F French in association with
    Sir John Burnet Tait & Partners
    (1949–53)

28. National Provincial Bank,
    St Andrew's Cross
    B C Sherren, staff architect to
    National Provincial Bank (1955–8)
    Listed Grade II

29. Pinnacle Quay flats, Harbour
    Avenue
    Form Design Group Architects
    (2004)

30. The Pavilions, Union Street/
    Millbay Road
    Module 2 Designers (1991)

31. King Street (later Wesley)
    Methodist Church, The Crescent
    Sir Percy Thomas & Son (1956–7,
    demolished c 2002)

32. Athenaeum, Derry's Cross
    Walls & Pearn (1958–61)

33. Royal Cinema (now Reel),
    Derry's Cross
    William R Glen (1936–8, damaged
    1941)

34. Barclays Bank, Armada Way/
    Notte Street
    W Curtis Green RA, Son & Lloyd
    (1949–52, altered 2006)
    Listed Grade II

35. Unitarian Church, Notte Street
    Louis de Soissons RA & Partners
    (1955–8)
    Listed Grade II

36. Baptist Church, Catherine Street
    Louis de Soissons RA & Partners
    (Louis de Soissons, Peacock,
    Hodges, Robertson & Fraser)
    (1956–9)
    Listed Grade II

37. Roman Catholic Church of
    Christ the King, Armada Way/
    Notte Street
    Sir Giles Scott, Son & Partner
    (1960–2)
    Listed Grade II

38. NAAFI (Navy, Army & Air Force
    Institutes) Services' Club, Notte
    Street/Armada Way
    Messrs Joseph (1949–51,
    demolished 2010)

39. Star flats, Notte Street
    H J W Stirling, city architect
    (c 1958)

40. Naval Memorial, the Hoe
    Sir Robert Lorimer (1920–4),
    Edward Maufe (post-1945)
    Listed Grade II

41. Tinside Lido, the Hoe
    W J Wibberley, city architect
    (1929–35)
    Listed Grade II